CW00555414

Reclaiming Christmas

Four Dimensions of Healing

Alexandra Walker

RECLAIMING CHRISTMAS

First edition. August 2023.

Copyright © 2023 Alexandra Walker, licensed to and published by Damsel Not In Distress Ltd.

Written by Alexandra Walker.

While every precaution has been taken in the preparation of this book, the publisher assumes no responsibility for errors or omissions, or for damages resulting from the use of the information contained herein.

Any information or guidance provided in this book is not a substitute for the consultation, diagnosis, and/or medical treatment of your doctor or healthcare provider. You must not rely on any information or guidance in this book as an alternative to medical advice from your doctor or healthcare provider and we expressly disclaim all responsibility, and shall have no liability, for any damages, loss, injury, or liability whatsoever suffered by you or any third party as a result of your reliance on any information or guidance in this book. If you have any specific questions or concerns about any medical matter, you should consult your doctor or healthcare provider as soon as possible. If you think you may be suffering from any medical condition, you should seek immediate medical attention from your healthcare provider. Do not delay seeking medical advice, disregard medical advice or discontinue medical treatment because of information or guidance in this book. Nothing in this disclaimer will limit or exclude any liability that may not be limited or excluded by applicable law.

Table of Contents

Preface 1

Prologue 5

Part One: How did I get here? 9

Chapter 1: What I have loved 11

Chapter 2: The perennial thundercloud 19

Chapter 3: Christmas as a Mount Everest of anxiety 31

Part Two: The seeds of hope 41

Chapter 4: Something in me can't give up 43

Chapter 5: I can't think my way out of this one 53

Chapter 6: Designing my own rituals 67

Part Three: The alchemy of my rituals 75

Chapter 7: Getting started 77

Chapter 8: Liberating my thinking mind 83

Chapter 9: Liberating my emotional mind 99

Chapter 10: Liberating my body 113

Chapter 11: Liberating my spirit 125

Chapter 12: Was all of this necessary? 137

Part Four: So how did my experiment turn out? 141

Chapter 13: Christmas 143

Chapter 14: What to do with the betwixt and between time? 149

Chapter 15: New Year – the part I had forgotten about 153

Chapter 16: The end of the season 159

Closing thoughts 163

Epilogue 165

References 167

About the Author 168

I dedicate this book to my faithful husband, Simon, and to my dear counsellor and friend, Ruth. Their unwavering love, support and wisdom were essential ingredients on my journey to becoming a Damsel Not In Distress.

Preface

Hello Dear Reader,
If you have chosen this book, it is perhaps because you are finding the prospect of Christmas difficult – and if that is so, I feel for you from the bottom of my heart. Or it may be because you know that a close family member or friend is struggling in this way.

As I write this preface, I too am in this unfortunate predicament. A season that used to be the pinnacle of my year has been rendered toxic, and at the moment it seems impossible for me to reclaim the joy and beauty that I once found in it. However, I'm a stubborn sort of gal and I refuse point blank to accept that this is the end of the story – for me or for you or for your friend. There has to be a better way...

And so, I'm embarking on an experiment, an actively designed programme of different approaches to discover how I can transform what has become a tarnished celebration.

For many people, it is grief of some kind which renders Christmas challenging. And no wonder – when we lose someone dear to us, with whom we have likely spent a number of joyous Christmases, it is incredibly tough to feel like celebrating without that person present with us anymore. Or perhaps the family with whom we have spent Christmas over a number of years is no more because of divorce. Or maybe we grieve the children we were never able to have. Traditions that used to bring us joy now serve as a bitter reminder of what we have lost. All the jollity may seem totally out of line with our grieving. And we may be lonely because we no longer have people around with whom to spend Christmas. All told, our emotions are likely to be all over the place, and this doesn't fit well with a season where everyone is focused on celebrating and enjoying themselves.

Grief and loss aren't the only reasons people find Christmas hard. Money can be a real source of angst, with all the intense pressure to buy the best things for other people. Or something bad might have happened during a previous Christmas, and the memories resurface each year. Or we may have to face an ongoing tough family relationship, which becomes all the tougher at Christmas time when we are supposed to cherish being with our family.

For me, the problem revolves around traumatic childhood experiences: emotional abuse, to baldly state the technical term. This was a widespread issue for me, affecting far more than Christmas, but here I am focusing on that season. I'm going to start this book by sharing with you my own experiences of emotional abuse, partly because I feel that these are issues that we still don't talk about enough. That's probably because they are deeply personal, and because they can make us feel ashamed. It's taken me years and years to fully comprehend and name what has happened to me, to accept that it is serious, and to affirm that it is not in any way my fault. This book does not describe that longer, more complex journey of realisation and healing – that's a story for another time – but it does look at how I have approached the reclamation of Christmas in the light of all those past events.

My sense is that emotional abuse is still often viewed as less serious than other forms of abuse and therefore surely fairly easy to overcome. I am fortunate enough not to have experienced other types of abuse, and am in no way questioning their horrible impacts. But I have learned through experience that childhood emotional abuse is serious in its own right.

It causes severe, long-term scarring. There are no easy answers, no quick-fix solutions. It takes considerable perseverance to identify and break through the invisible barriers and defence mechanisms that have understandably been built up. And it takes even more effort to realise that your belief systems have been messed up by what happened. And more effort still to work towards seeing the world from a fresh, healthier perspective.

I want to share my story to give voice to voiceless others in similar situations, but also so that you understand the depths of the challenges I'm facing. I certainly have deep-seated issues with Christmas. I hope that, if you also find Christmas challenging, you will find help and inspiration in the pages of this book, even if the source of your difficulty is not the same as mine.

I am also aware that there are other traditions and celebrations that might throw up similar challenges: Hanukkah, Diwali, Eid Al-Fitr, to name but a few, and indeed any number of events which are marked by tradition, gatherings and memories of the past. For example, I can also find my birthday tricky because of the pressure for it to be a good day, and past family associations which render it complex. Again, I believe that, whilst this book is focused around Christmas, it will prove helpful for those with difficulties relating to another event with similar characteristics.

I don't offer a one size fits all, cookie cutter, 100% guaranteed approach to healing, but rather a way of approaching it that I hope you can use and adapt to your own circumstances and preferences. However deep our wounds, I believe that there are ways that we can journey through to the light, ways that we can heal and transform beyond our wildest imaginings. And I want to inspire you that, if this is possible for me, it can also be possible for you! Of course, I can't be sure at this stage whether my experiment will work – but I feel a gentle knowing that all will be well. Let's see what unfolds...

A free resource to accompany this book

I've put together *Your Ideal Christmas Present*, a five-day video course designed to help you reconnect with what you really love about Christmas. It's free! Please do visit my website at www.damselnotindistress.co.uk/xmasfreebie to get hold of it.

Prologue

Walking alone down a dark Scottish country lane at 11:30pm on Christmas Eve 2012, I felt strangely at peace. I had escaped the madness. I had taken control, for once.

I loved walking, the steady rhythm of it, the reassuring feeling of the ground beneath my feet. It was there whenever I needed it, supporting me with every step. It stabilised me, calmed my frazzled nerves.

I felt the crisp, chilly winter air on my face, like a refreshing splash of cold water. I drew it into my lungs, stressed and shallow at first. Breath by breath, I calmed as I purposefully walked away from the thing I hated.

There were no streetlights, but I remember being able to see enough to make my way. I didn't need a torch. I had always been rather dubious of the dark, but this felt benign, comforting.

There was no noise, no one about. That was comforting too. My mind had been filled to the brim with crazy, hurtful words that night. Silence was a balm to my soul.

I couldn't tell you how long I walked for – probably not long at all, but it felt spacious in some ways, as well as totally alien. I could walk out into the dark by myself and figure out what to do. Help would emerge. I would be safe. Turns out that was a much bigger metaphor than I realised at the time.

But I was in uncharted territory. I didn't know where I was going, beyond a rough knowledge that I would come upon a small village after several miles. I had my phone in my pocket but no one to call. My husband was with his family and I couldn't contemplate disturbing them. (I look back on that thought with wonder – of course my loving husband would have wanted me to ring him in such a situation!)

I genuinely had no idea if I would ever go back home – well, no, it wasn't my home, it was my parents' home. Mummy desperately wanted me to think of it as my home, but that ship had sailed a while ago.

That year, she had just had a massive cancerous growth removed from her tummy – ovarian cancer which would take her away from us sooner than we realised at the time. The signs that in retrospect looked rather like flashing red lights on a dashboard had been ignored and misinterpreted for months – too long, as it turned out.

So perhaps to an outsider it would be natural that my father had become angry on Christmas Eve, venting his frustration at a truly scary situation that threatened to take away the one who had been his constant companion for forty years. Maybe so, but it was a pattern of behaviour that had driven me over the edge this time. I knew how few Christmases we might have left together, so why stab me again with those sharp, hurtful words?

I couldn't tell you much about the argument, it was all so meaningless. But very, very hurtful. There was an oft-repeated theme about all the problems with "my generation" somewhere in the mix. My father knew just what to say and how to say it for maximum effect. It's ironic, therefore, that I can't remember most of what was said. Even so, each hurtful word left an indelible mark on my body and on my soul.

My only vivid memory of that argument is in the kitchen. I sank to the floor on my knees, screaming that I wasn't going to do this again. It was a primal response from an only child who had put up with such things for way too long. As a girl, I had frozen in the face of such anger, waiting and praying for it to blow over. More recently, I had sometimes wrestled with it, confident in the strength and honesty of my defence – but that hadn't worked either.

So that night I just walked purposefully away, and it felt good. It felt powerful and decisive.

As I walked down the road contemplating my next move, the glare of car headlights suddenly appeared behind me. It was my father coming to pick me up. My time of exerting power was over, or so it seemed. I assumed he had come to his senses and would apologise for all the unnecessary hurt and distress he had caused.

We drove back home in silence. The wheels crunched on the gravel of the driveway and we stopped. I will never forget what happened next.

My father turned to me and said, "So, are you ready to give in yet?"

Inwardly, my soul wrenched in shock and bitter disappointment. The battle was not over. His only child leaving the house in the middle of the night had not been enough to shock him out of his crazy mood. Would I ever find the key?

Outwardly, I just looked back calmly and said that word an insubordinate toddler loves to say: No.

I went up to my room and contemplated just how awful this Christmas Eve was proving to be. We had always rescued things in the past – just. But I couldn't see it this time. There didn't seem to be any way back from the brink. My stomach churned.

Then suddenly Mummy appeared at the door: "Daddy would like to see you." Really, I thought? With a truckload of trepidation, I headed downstairs. Then suddenly I found myself sitting on my father's knee – rather too big and grown up for that now, but it happened anyway. Dazed and confused, I heard him say, "You do know that I love you, don't you?" Mummy stated the blindingly obvious: "Well no, I don't think she does know that right now, Daddy." It was one of her finest moments of honest clarity.

All of a sudden, the storm was over as quickly as it had started. Like a tornado wreaking havoc and then vanishing from sight. I sat there, totally bewildered, wondering what on earth could have happened to effect this transformation. Had Mummy conjured up some magic words to convince him to stop? Had his brain suddenly flipped back to what I liked to consider was his normal state?

I would never know the answer to that question. I wasn't given the opportunity to ask what on earth had just happened, to heal properly. Was there an apology? I honestly don't remember, but I don't believe so. Direct apologies weren't generally in my father's repertoire.

My mind was racing. I knew only too well what was expected of me now. I needed to come off the rollercoaster because my father was ready for it to stop. I didn't want to. I really, really didn't want to. It felt unjust, wrong, deeply hurtful. I wanted to keep fighting the good fight. But I looked at Mummy and knew I had no choice but to save Christmas for her. After all, she may not have many Christmases left...

We salvaged it. It must have been so late by the time we went to bed, and even later when I could finally snatch some kind of fitful sleep. But we arose the next morning and enacted Christmas the way we always had. Mummy was stuffing the turkey first thing in the morning, and then we opened presents while dinner was cooking.

I was totally overwrought, but I played my part as best I could. I even made sure we got a family photo at the dinner table, although it took several attempts to get a shot where we all looked tolerably happy. Mummy and I gave each other our customary stockings, with the presents that we had spent all year gathering thoughtfully from different places. We had scraped through once again, but at what cost?

Part One: How did I get here?

In which I describe how, as someone who loved Christmas so much, I landed up dreading and then totally avoiding the festive season.

Chapter 1: What I have loved

I have always loved the beauty, the joy, the magical feeling that Christmas brings. I think I must have inherited that from Mummy. She adored the specialness of the season. She spent all year gathering up thoughtful presents and stashing them away, and planning for all the different traditions.

It feels like all sorts of amazing things are possible which wouldn't seem reasonable at other times of year. I loved Father Christmas; he was kind and generous to me. I even got to speak to him on the phone one Christmas Eve, although he never said anything to me, he only talked to Daddy. I used to get nervous about whether Father Christmas would know where we were going to be, so I would write him a letter to let him know. And I remember my amazement each year when the mince pie had been eaten and the brandy drunk – how had I not heard him?

One Christmas Eve at my grandparents' house in Bristol, I was doing my best to get to – and stay – asleep. Always a challenge! Then, when I was absolutely certain that everyone had settled down for the night, I suddenly heard the magical tinkle of bells breaking the silence. I lay stock still in bed, amazed by chills of wonderment – was it ... could it really be ... yes it just had to be the bells on Father Christmas' sleigh!! Goodness only knows how I managed to sleep after that. And goodness only knows how my parents ever managed to fill my stocking without waking me up. It's one of those golden, shining memories that doesn't fade when a lot of other ones gradually drift out of one's mind over time.

Like many excited kids, I would jump into my parents' bed pretty early on Christmas morning, so unbelievably excited to open my stocking. I would love all the little presents that were infused with thoughtfulness and imagination – and I would perhaps grow increasingly curious over the years as to how Father Christmas seemed to have done his shopping in the exact same places that my parents had travelled that year! But of course, reasoned Mummy, it was because she had given him recommendations when she saw things she knew I'd love. Which was quite enough to satisfy me for a while longer. I was in no hurry to give up the notion of a benevolent old man whose whole existence centred around making children happy. Even when I had no choice but to wake up to the reality, I carried on pretending – because why not?

There was a tradition that I would find a small present at my place setting at dinner on Christmas Eve. One year when I was eight or nine, I was astonished to find a cute little baby reindeer looking plaintively up at me. He was quite simply adorable: floppy felt antlers, gorgeously soft fur, a bright red nose (of course) and a quite angelic face. It was love at first sight. I christened him Yuli, after a character in a TV show we'd been watching. Apparently, Yuli was Rudolph's grandson, and he was meant to be helping to pull Father Christmas' sleigh that year. But he was rather too small, and he'd had a bit of an accident and fallen off the sleigh, landing right onto my grandparents' roof! Luckily, he wasn't hurt, but unfortunately he hadn't been able to get back to the sleigh. He seemed surprisingly unbothered by the incident, and was just so grateful to be able to join a loving family. Yuli is still a big part of my life now. Turns out he's quite the rogue, but that's a story for another time...!

I was an only child with quite a small extended family, but people made an effort so that I had a goodly number of presents to open. I always had one main present from my parents. I'll always remember the year Daddy kept telling me my big present was three inches long by two inches wide – and I pondered how on earth my big present could be so tiny. It turned out to be the biggest present I'd ever received! I felt such joy and excitement as Mummy carefully carried the huge parcel down the stairs on Christmas morning, and was enthralled when I opened it! (In case you're wondering, it was an early generation children's computer, with a screen that would seem very small by today's standards.)

My aunt Dorothy had quite the habit of spoiling me with endless presents – she loved to make Christmas special for me, having not been able to have children of her own. I remember the zenith was when she proudly produced fourteen presents for me – fourteen! I don't remember now what they all were, but I do recall opening one parcel to find a lovely hot water bottle with a soft pink cover. I was always a chilly child, so I loved the idea of something I could cuddle safely, without it burning me. Then, a bit later on, I came across a parcel that looked surprisingly similar in shape. I ripped off the paper...and what a surprise, there was another hot water bottle, this time with a blue cover! I was slightly discombobulated, but then wondered if perhaps Dorothy wanted to give me one for when I was travelling. But no – in reality, she looked rather taken aback, and said she'd bought the other hot water bottle for herself and must have wrapped it by mistake. I loved that moment, such wonderful honesty!

Traditions emerged over the years, with Mummy's love of putting in effort to make Christmas special rubbing off on me. In the time before digital photographs and easy online ways of creating calendars, I made my parents a monthly calendar with coloured card and printed photos that Mummy had given me of our holidays that year. My parents adored having that calendar up in their office, reminding them of fun times. And so, a new tradition was born, as it became customary for me to make them each a calendar every year.

I also learned how to make Christmas crackers with toilet roll holders, crepe paper, curling ribbon, and snappers to create the all-important satisfying 'bang' when they were pulled. I spent ages searching out imaginative gifts that were small enough to fit inside. There were always plenty of funny wind-up toys, bouncy balls and little puzzles. I particularly remember some slimy guy that you could fling at the wall, and he would rather grotesquely slither down, in such a way that you couldn't take your eyes off him. I bought joke books and searched out proper, laugh-out-loud entries, rather than the rather questionable jokes you often find in Christmas crackers. And I even made a hat to go inside each one. I lovingly assembled each cracker and added a beautiful sticker to decorate the finished product. I would hide them in my room and bring them down to much acclaim for Christmas lunch. I gave a lot of joy and laughter with those crackers, and we had a blast pulling them after the ritual feast of turkey and all the trimmings.

As I grew older, I didn't like the idea of losing out on a stocking filled with prezzies! So of course, Mummy continued to give me one, but now that I was older, I wouldn't rush into my parents' room to open it at silly o'clock in the morning... One year, I had a genius idea. I bought a beautiful stocking with a gorgeous teddy's face at the top, with his paws folding over to close it up. Well, that was the idea anyway. By the time I'd filled it with presents for Mummy, poor teddy had quite the job holding all those presents in! In fact, one or two of the presents were just too large and had to sit alongside the stocking. I brought it down on Christmas Day when Mummy was busy in the kitchen and hung it in the living room. I'll never forget how enchanted and surprised she was when she saw it! Naturally, that became a new tradition, and Mummy did so love her teddy stocking.

I adored carol singing: such beautiful, evocative music that stirred my soul, and another beloved tradition. I lived for the school carol service, for which the choir practised from about September. I was lucky enough to have been blessed with a pure chorister's voice, and so I got the chance to sing solos sometimes, hearing my voice soaring up to the high church roof. At university, that experience culminated with opening the service with the first verse of *Once in Royal David's City*. The stunning chapel was crammed full of students wanting to be part of the special occasion. I led the choir in and stood under the archway for a couple of minutes before we got started – just enough time to feel prickles of nerves in my stomach. But then the time came and I rose to the occasion, revelling in every second of it as my voice didn't waver or let me down. What a privilege.

I also composed my own songs. I had no idea where this ability came from, but it just started to happen after I'd played the piano for a few years. And what could be more natural than writing Christmas carols? I had several of my creations performed at my school's carol service, which was a feeling quite unlike anything else I had experienced. To create something original, that was an expression of myself, and have it brought to life and shared with others was truly magical.

Food obviously played a major role in the whole event. Of course, we had special treats that we only indulged in at this time of year. Chocolate Yule log, rose and violet creams, and Turkish delight were all perennial favourites in our household, tempered with a goodly number of tangerines to make it all feel a tad less unhealthy! We boiled a ham on Christmas Eve, and Mummy made her signature winter salad – gala apples, beetroot and celery. She persisted in including the celery, even though Daddy and I tried to eat it all first or even just leave it on the side in favour of the sweeter alternatives. She always ordered an extraordinarily large turkey, and it took us quite a few days to chomp our way through it in various guises. Homemade stuffing required a prodigious quantity of breadcrumbs and fresh parsley. And then there was bubble and squeak on Boxing Day, later complemented by a Scottish dish called skirlie made by Daddy, which was a moreish combination of oatmeal, onions and a generous amount of fat.

Decorations sparkled everywhere. Mummy and I would put them up as soon as we felt it was decent to do so in the run-up to Christmas. I loved the shiny tinsel adorning picture frames and mirrors, and all the decorations that had been gathered lovingly over the years. There was a skiing scene with little characters that my grandfather had made for Mummy. There was a very old Father Christmas who sat on the dining table like a kindly benefactor. There were snow globes, cute little animals, and an angelic set of choristers. There was a lovely house that lit up. There was a Christmas tree with decorations garnered from family and from various holidays over the years, and a gorgeous robin at the top which came from Mummy's family. There were Christmas placemats, napkins, even festive loo roll! And then there were those shepherds I had made with Mummy at pre-school nursery – kitchen roll holder bodies, bits of fabric for robes, and cotton wool for beards. Not much to look at if you didn't know their history, but infused with mother-daughter love and creativity.

I revelled in the warm and fuzzy feeling of Christmas. I loved nothing more than to snuggle up with Mummy in our cosy living room watching a seasonal film. Those films where magic actually happens, where miracles that would seem totally out of reach at other times of year come together just in time for Christmas. Those films where the ending is not in doubt, but you enjoy going along for the ride and getting caught up in that world of shining possibility. Of course elves exist and can save the day, of course Cinderella gets to go to the ball, of course two unlikely people could fall in love at Christmas and live happily ever after. Of course the magic gets to happen!

Chapter 2: The perennial thundercloud

S o, after all that, you might wonder what all the fuss is about. I clearly loved Christmas with all its various bells and whistles, so why all the drama?

Tragically, amidst all the sparkle, laughter and fun, a dark Thundercloud would descend at some point in the run-up to Christmas Day. I don't recall when it first made an appearance, but I do remember painfully that it became a regular fixture.

It would generally start at the dinner table, probably encouraged by the ever-present alcohol. Mummy would have prepared one of her special pre-Christmas meals. Perhaps I would sense that my father's mood was off at the start of the conversation, or perhaps Mummy or I would say something and I would instantly detect the change in mood. Once that had happened, there was no rescuing the situation. The Thundercloud had set in, and it would stay until such time as my father decided that it could dissipate.

The Thundercloud came in slightly different forms. Sometimes it was a flash in the pan. An argument flared up over something – goodness knows what, I genuinely don't remember any more. There would be a veritable wall of angry words, cutting comments, and nasty insinuations. Voices were raised and I was scared. Sometimes I was an active participant, at other times more of an observer as my parents wrangled and fought over something. By the next morning, it had all blown over. This left me dazed and confused – I never slept when there had been arguing in the house, but then suddenly things were cheery again and I was expected to get with the programme. There were never any meaningful conversations about what had happened, no explaining to little Alexandra what it had all been about, no reassuring her that it wasn't her fault.

But more often than not, the Thundercloud was worse than a flash in the pan: either a bigger explosion, or an insidious, rumbling low mood. At times like these, the consequences reverberated for longer. When the situation finally improved, there would be a fragile atmosphere, a nervous tension in the house as my father seemed to have settled down but could not by any stretch of the imagination be described as jolly. The Christmas decorations were up, but the festive spirit was most certainly absent. Mummy and I would gingerly go about our day, trying not to aggravate the situation further. Slowly but surely, the Thundercloud would lift.

And so it was that Christmas Day itself was always a success – in the sense that we went through our traditions, and did our best to enjoy them. But the problem was that I began to develop more and more of a gnawing dread about how we would get there. I would walk on eggshells in the run-up to Christmas, being achingly sure of the inevitability of the Thundercloud, but not knowing exactly how or when it would strike. Would I be the one to cause its appearance? Was there anything I could do to stop this calamity from happening? These were questions that chewed away at me increasingly over time. I believe I would have done almost anything to prevent it.

As I got older, I began to muse as to whether there was any underlying reason for my father's pre-Christmas malaise. Had he lost someone special just before Christmas one year? Or was there some other dreadful memory that plagued him? Or was it quite simply that he didn't really resonate with Christmas and couldn't muster the necessary joy all of the time? Of course, he could be unpleasant at any time of year, but why was it reliably so much worse in that supposedly festive season? Whatever the cause – and I will probably never uncover it now – it was clear that he needed an outlet for some pent-up rage, and those closest to him were neatly in the line of fire.

By this time, I had come to appreciate just how much Christmas meant to Mummy. She struggled hugely with the darkness and stress of the world, and Christmas was the magical time where she could make the light shine. So you can imagine how difficult and tragic she found it each time the Thundercloud appeared. And therefore I would do anything in my power to make things right for her, even if it meant swallowing how I felt, or going along with a makeshift truce in order to get back on track to Christmas as it should be, as she longed for it to be. However, the stakes began to get higher as I got older, until eventually Christmas became a veritable magnet for disaster.

Shortly after I got married to Simon at the tender age of 23, we went to my parents' house for Christmas, and it was the first time that Simon was exposed to the full power of my father's wrath. I had suffered from chronic insomnia for several years: its roots stemmed from my childhood and it was one of a number of troubling health conditions which bubbled up as I grew older. I would literally lie awake for hours, sometimes only getting a couple of fitful hours of what could generously be described as sleep before I had to get up and face another inexorable day. I was really struggling. I had tried everything I could find to make the situation better – and I had identified that certain factors helped me, like regular exercise, and others had a serious detrimental effect. My back was prone to what I described as "sickening aches" which didn't seem to be relieved by anything – and hard, unyielding beds made that problem significantly worse. I'm slender and fairly light, and hard beds felt like lying on concrete.

My parents had recently bought a new double bed for the spare room. It was ridiculously hard. After a brutal first night of restlessness and pain, I knew I couldn't cope. I was beside myself – what on earth could I do about this situation? Simon suggested we talk to my parents about it, but I was way too frightened to do that. It was perhaps 21st

December, and mentioning this problem would cause friction which would almost certainly lead to the appearance of the Thundercloud. But I also simply couldn't cope with the idea of facing Christmas in such trying circumstances. I wouldn't be able to keep myself together when the inevitable difficulties occurred. My reserves would be totally depleted, and who knew what calamity could unfold if I didn't have my wits about me?

Simon was a bit mystified by the situation, but concocted an alternative plan. We would go out on a pretext, visit a bed shop, find a better mattress and arrange for it to be delivered as soon as possible before Christmas. When we got back home, the situation would be a *fait accompli* which my father couldn't resist or undo. Forgiveness is easier than permission, and all that. We enacted the plan, but I felt that familiar gnawing dread as we drove home.

My father didn't respond well to the news. He was confused, frustrated. What was he supposed to do with the existing mattress? Wasn't this all a bit drastic? My insomnia and Simon's desire to help me didn't seem to be his primary concerns. I made one fatal mistake as the conversation unfolded. I got upset – understandable for someone who had hardly slept the night before. I told Mummy just how bad my sleeping problems were, and how I was finding it really hard to carry on with life under these circumstances.

That comment cut Mummy to the quick. I don't know exactly how the conversation unfolded between my parents, because Simon and I went upstairs and sheltered in our room. But I surely felt the consequences of it. My father burst into our room and angrily said that I had no right to upset my mother in that way, and that if I wasn't going to help him keep her cheerful, then I could f*** off. The angry conversation continued and I had nowhere to run. Nothing I said made the situation any better. There was no concern for my inability to sleep, for my welfare, no consideration of what had driven us to such great lengths.

Now I know that, on one level, my father was driven by his concern for Mummy and her feelings. There was no doubt that she became easily depressed and he did a lot to keep her afloat. But it was a horrible encounter in which seemingly he couldn't have empathy for both of his nearest and dearest at the same time. I recall with absolute clarity just how scared I felt: even when I had tried to solve a real, physical problem in the best way I could muster, the Thundercloud had still emerged. And the finger of blame was firmly pointed in my direction: this one was on me.

Simon had sat stock still during this tirade, totally stunned. Afterwards, he was horrified at the aggression, so upset to see what I was up against. I comforted him, and told him that I knew how wrong the relationship was. In that moment of lucidity, I told him that Mummy was the sole reason I stuck around in this dysfunctional family set-up. I explained that the only way I knew to manage the Thundercloud was to allow it to blow over, and not further antagonise my father. Simon told me that he still wanted to stay with me, despite having seen the full horror of the situation, and agreed to follow my lead in how to minimise the conflicts. Years later, he told me that he had clung to my moment of lucidity, as his assurance that I knew the truth of the situation even if I couldn't bear to talk about it again, and as his restraint when he desperately wanted to take me away from it.

And so the pattern rumbled on. Simon was now as wary as I was of the Thundercloud, and we navigated our way through as best we could. At least I now had a partner in crime. There's nothing more lonely than being an only child when your parents are fighting. There was no one to talk to, to distract me, to reassure me. Now I had Simon sitting next to me at the dining table, a firm, loving presence. When the inevitable Thundercloud emerged, he could support me through it, sit with me through the dark hours, and carry me to the other side with less permanent scarring...

On a more normal matter, we decided, as many couples do, to alternate Christmases between our two families, and would always go and see the other family for a late Christmas and New Year celebration. Interestingly, I began to discern a pattern that those late Christmases with my parents tended to go much better. In fact, on occasion the Thundercloud didn't actually appear – what a miracle! Perhaps there was just less pressure on the situation, even though we were doing exactly the same things, following the same rituals, but just a couple of days behind the customary schedule.

However, things took a turn for the worse when Mummy got sick, culminating in the sheer disaster of Christmas 2012 that I described at the start of this book.

The next year, Mummy was in remission from the ovarian cancer and her specialist was hopeful. I wrangled with what to do about Christmas. I had spent the last two Christmases with my family, but Mummy had been through so much, so perhaps we should do that again? Alternatively, was it now right to spend the day with Simon's family, especially as his dad had suffered from Parkinson's disease for many years and therefore also faced an uncertain future. I had endless phone calls with my parents talking this through, and Mummy reassured me that I should spend Christmas with Simon's family, and that she would love to see me directly afterwards.

And so that was what we did. Again, no Thundercloud that year, fitting into my hypothesis that doing Christmas slightly out of sync took the pressure off. But little did I know that this would come to be used against me – Christmas would be wielded as the ultimate weapon of guilt and shame, to brutalise my emotions on another poignant occasion.

Roll forward a couple of months, and tragically Mummy's cancer had returned with a vengeance. Reading between the lines of the careful statements made by her specialist, the prognosis was not good. She eventually succumbed to the illness in July. It was devastating, she was most certainly taken "too soon" – she was 64 and I was 33. I had lost the Mummy who had loved me so much. Her close friends told me that I had been her world.

The Scottish Borders were ridiculously sunny – the kind of weather that literally hardly ever happens up there – and I was angry because the bright blue skies felt so incongruent with my grieving. Simon and I stayed with my father the week after Mummy died. It was of course cruelly hard for him. He loved her fiercely, they had been together for over forty years, and suddenly his world had fallen apart.

Grief is complicated and messy and personal. But his grief was far more damaging than necessary, to him and to me. The behaviours that made him difficult at any time, and especially at times of emotion, went into deep, brooding over-drive. He spent long hours in silence sitting in the garden, Then he would often become argumentative and loud in the evenings. Simon and I generally retreated to our room at that point, scared to interact with him in that mood, lest he say or do something awful or provoke us into a response. Sometimes he wrote angry notes and shoved them under our door, but we didn't come out. The risks were too high.

It all came to a head the day before Mummy's funeral. Simon and I had gone out for a walk, and when we returned, my father's mood had drastically changed. I prickled. This was not good news. And on this occasion, I couldn't get away in time. He became very angry at me, telling me that Mummy couldn't believe that I hadn't spent last Christmas with her. She had woken up on Christmas Day so sad, disappointed and hurt that I wasn't there to share it with her. And it had been her last Christmas. How on earth could I have done that to her? How selfish and thoughtless was I as a daughter?

In that moment, Christmas became the ultimate weapon of guilt and shame. And it was pointed directly at me, to hurt me in the most emotionally charged week of my life.

I couldn't take it. I wouldn't take it. It was grossly unfair, mean-spirited and downright cruel of him. He knew exactly how to make me hurt, which weapon to use, and he had no compunction in using that knowledge to its greatest effect. Of course, I couldn't speak to Mummy about what he had said. I couldn't ask her if this allegation was true. I couldn't hear her reassure me, or apologise to her and make amends if I had in fact hurt her. It was a missile calculated for maximum emotional damage, and I couldn't wait around to see how much worse the ammunition could get.

I had to leave the house, driven out by his sheer anger and vitriol. He told us that we weren't welcome at the funeral the next day. Simon and I hurriedly packed our things and drove away, escaping with no idea of what would happen next.

I am painfully aware that we left my father on his own, a grieving husband on the day before his wife's funeral. But we weren't safe – with Mummy no longer with us, I feared where his rage might lead him, or us. And I could not take that level of targeted anger any more – indeed, I had just lost the one reason why I had put up with it for all those years. And I should not have had to take it in that moment – after all, I was grieving too.

Even though this took place during the height of the summer holidays, Simon and I found one bed and breakfast room available – "the only vacancy for six weeks", the owner proudly declared, before quickly recognising how distraught we were and giving us everything we needed without fuss.

The next morning, my father got in touch. It had the feel of previous 'mornings after the fight before'. He said of course we were welcome at the funeral. When we met up at the crematorium, things were a little different to previous occasions: he apologised, the only time I can firmly remember that happening. We said goodbye to Mummy in a quiet way. It was just the three of us there, the way my father wanted it. I sang *Amazing Grace* a cappella, a fitting song indeed for such a turbulent period.

The apology didn't last though. I really should have seen that one coming. Starting not long afterwards, my father would comment out of the blue that, whilst I generally had very good judgement, he could think of one time when I had shown very poor judgement. He was pointedly referring to me leaving him that day before the funeral. I made it very clear the few times he uttered those words that I was not prepared to have that conversation, and just about enabled us to move on. But he was still trying to make me feel as if what had happened was my fault. And on several levels, he was succeeding, even if I had a growing sense that what was going on was not right.

After Mummy's death, we had a few unconventional Christmases trying to get used to life without her. Times abroad doing completely different things proved relatively successful when we were together. I felt terrible guilt and worry, however, the first Christmas when my father was by himself and went to Paris while I hosted Simon's family. It was my dream to host Christmas, and to do things beautifully and thoughtfully the way Mummy had done, whilst putting my own twist on it. My husband even secretly arranged for loads of my friends to contribute gifts to give me the most enormous Christmas stocking I had ever had – which was incredible!

But late on Christmas Day I got a heart-rending message from my father about how awful life was without Mummy. I was so guilty and concerned that I mobilised myself and spent a few hours of Boxing Day with him in Paris. We actually really enjoyed the lights and the atmosphere, and had a lovely steak dinner, but he insisted that I go straight back home after a short night's sleep. I arrived back home and took up my hostess responsibilities again having hardly missed a beat. But I was emotionally exhausted.

In 2018, I had a second chance to host Christmas for Simon's family, but it was blighted by the dreaded norovirus. This first struck the youngest member of our party on the 23rd, then spread to almost all members of the family on Christmas Eve. All my fun plans and projects were well and truly scuppered. While I was the only one not to fall physically sick, it was another stab in the heart, another missed opportunity for a magical Christmas.

So, in 2019, I wanted to try something different with my father, something to evoke the real spirit of Christmas. Knowing that going away had worked well in the past, I decided to try and make a dream of mine a reality – staying in a snowy wonderland for Christmas. My father would obviously have preferred somewhere hot, but he acquiesced to the plan, and we alighted on Switzerland. I found a gorgeous, swanky hotel with a luxury spa and an outdoor thermal pool overlooking in the mountains. I was over the moon. This had to be a winning formula.

We arrived in the late afternoon and were welcomed personally. The view from our rooms was beautiful, although there wasn't as much snow as I had hoped for – but hey ho, you can't have everything.

Everything unravelled a couple of hours later. I was totally unprepared.

We went for dinner and it didn't go so well. The details don't matter – suffice to say that there was some poor service and a rather sullen waiter. The sort of stuff that would not have mattered to me given the specialness of the festivities and surroundings. But with my father there, I felt waves of sickness as the situation unfolded and I could automatically sense the Thundercloud coming into view. I excused myself from the table and cried panic-stricken, stressful tears in the bathroom. How could this have happened again? Why had I tried to make my Christmas dream come true when it was always going to be doomed to failure?

I spent the night feeling awful and sleeping little, inwardly pleading that the staff would placate my father somehow. But the next morning senior management were not particularly interested in his complaint. The tragic consequence was that we were trapped in a hotel for nearly a week where he was palpably grumpy much of the time, and from which there was no means of escape.

Although the snow fell the next day, almost as if on cue for the Christmas celebrations, it didn't bring nearly as much pleasure as I had hoped. My father drank too much daily and, having given up on the hotel restaurant for obvious reasons, we ran the gauntlet of eating out. While some of it went quite well, much of it didn't. I was tense at the prospect of him being loud and overbearing, and embarrassed when it happened. And whenever I felt like we might be making some progress towards greater equanimity, the Thundercloud descended again. I have rarely felt so sick in my life.

We did manage to have a nice time on Christmas morning, taking a cable car up a mountain and walking back down the snowy mountainside – that was basically my only happy memory of the week, and again I was doing it out of some compulsion to make a 'success' out of Christmas Day itself.

I hoped that this better mood might continue into Boxing Day to somewhat retrieve the situation, but I was sadly mistaken. I knocked on my father's door to go out for dinner, and he was totally inebriated. Not just a little tipsy, but completely and utterly drunk. I simply couldn't face the prospect of navigating dinner, so I thought on my feet and I lied. I don't tell lies easily, but that night I could see no choice. I said that I had an upset tummy and so I wouldn't be able to go to dinner. Well, it turns out that it wasn't that much of a lie, as it was absolutely true that my stomach was churning – with fear and dread. The next morning, we left Switzerland, trying to pretend with strained smiles that it had all been a great success.

By this point, Christmas had been damaged for me so many times that I was at the point of no return, although I didn't fully appreciate that yet...

Chapter 3: Christmas as a Mount Everest of anxiety

The recurring Thunderclouds that I have faced, at Christmas and more widely, have left me with what feels like permanent scarring. This scarring has manifested itself in a few different ways.

Always on the alert for danger

Imagine you always got whacked on the head by a rubber mallet that materialised out of nowhere, at roughly the same time each year. There was nothing you could do to anticipate exactly when it would appear, or to prevent it from whacking you. The whack always gave you a massive headache that lasted at least a day, sometimes quite a bit longer.

You'd come to expect it. You'd come to dread it. You'd look suspiciously at anything else that tended to happen at that time of year – surely it was more than coincidence, perhaps you could find the cause of the whacking if you looked hard enough? Those coincidental events would also become tainted with the mallet's whack, because your clever brain would make the association and so you'd think of pain when you thought of those things. And the more often the mallet appeared, the stronger that association would become.

In fact, you can almost imagine a film where the protagonist always gets whacked on his birthday, every year without fail. He tries different strategies and tactics, with greater degrees of desperation as the film progresses, to figure out where the mallet comes from and to foil it in its dastardly deed. Of course, ironically, these attempts to avert the attack totally mess up his birthday every year in darkly comedic ways. Now this is a film we're talking about, so the protagonist would surely succeed after much travail and make things good. The mallet would be subdued or outfoxed somehow, and the protagonist would live happily ever after, finally able to enjoy his birthday in peace.

But what about back in the real world where happy endings are less assured? What if the mallet just kept striking? And even if it did eventually stop for some reason, would that immediately herald the arrival of happily ever after?

Over the years, I developed a dread of the Thundercloud appearing, a dread that would totally colour the run-up to Christmas. I became hyper-sensitive to my father's moods, vigilant for the first sign of the Thundercloud's arrival. As a young child, the apparent lack of logic was completely bewildering to me. But as I gathered evidence over the years, I began to understand it at least a little better. Perhaps if I just spotted the Thundercloud quickly enough, I could avert it somehow. Having seemingly started an argument in a previous year with a careless choice of words, perhaps I could do better next time. So, when my father next brought up a contentious topic at the dining table, if I had my wits about me, I would not say what I really thought if I believed that it might antagonise him in his current state. I would guard my words in the hope of not being the one to flip the switch.

Sometimes I would feel able to relax a little more, if he was jovial and things were going well. But I also knew that things could change almost in an instant with the wrong combination of inputs. And there was one input in particular that I couldn't control...

A wariness of the booze

As a young child, my father's unpredictable behaviour would thoroughly confuse me. How could the Daddy who was so lovely and caring one minute suddenly turn into an angry monster? As I grew older, I noticed that alcohol was a key contributing factor. Watching many people get tipsy can be rather amusing, as alcohol simply makes them drop their inhibitions and giggle rather more than would normally be considered usual! But in some people, like my father, alcohol amplifies an inherent aggression and brings it surging to the surface. Suddenly it feels like you are dealing with a completely different person, and one who doesn't have much in the way of control.

I became aware of the story of Jekyll and Hyde by Robert Louis Stevenson, and it seemed to fit the bill rather well. Dr Jekyll was a kind, clever and respected scientist – but he also wanted to bring out his "second" nature. So, using his scientific knowledge, he was able to concoct a potion which would do just that. He could take a walk on the dark side without having to bear responsibility for what happened. His alter ego Hyde carried out various nefarious deeds, including assault and murder.

I won't spoil the story any further, in case you haven't read it and want to dive in! But clearly this story resonated with me – substitute alcohol for the potion, and angry, cutting words for physical violence, and the metaphor held pretty well.

But uncovering this connection didn't do me much good, except to make me even more on the alert for the Thundercloud after the booze began to flow. Whilst Mummy occasionally had some success in moderating how much and what my father imbibed, this was something that I couldn't control in the slightest. This was an issue at any time of year, but more so at Christmas.

I do remember starting to hate the appearance of that crystal cut glass whose contents shone with a rich amber hue, because it signified that anything could happen from that point onwards...

Fight, flight, freeze or fawn?

You are probably aware of the fight or flight responses – if a threat turns up, your instincts either lead you to engage the enemy in combat, or to run away as fast as you can. Now we may like to think that we make a conscious decision, but in reality this is all pretty automated stuff which emanates from the least evolved part of our brain. Some fondly call this our "lizard brain". Think of an animal being attacked by another creature – when the threat appears, it weighs up the odds quickly and subconsciously. If it thinks it is bigger and stronger than the other creature, it will likely stick around and fight. But if it reckons it can outpace its opponent, it may well decide to run away. All pretty logical stuff so far.

But I had learned to my cost that the fight response didn't work for me when the Thundercloud appeared. I remember clearly the day when I chalked up that particular life lesson. I was perhaps ten years old and Mummy, Daddy and I were playing Monopoly. Daddy had taken on the role of the banker – an oft contested decision because it gave the chosen one greater access to those piles of precious coloured banknotes. I was a sharp kid with a fiercely logical mathematical brain, and it became blindingly obvious to me that my father had taken additional money from the bank during the opening rounds of the game. He just couldn't have accumulated that much cash at that point in the game, having paid for the properties he now proudly brandished.

It is always tough playing board games against one's parents – I often lost until I developed greater skill as I got older, plus I had no siblings to practise with, so it really was just me pitted against my older and wiser parents. I have also always had a huge compulsion to speak the truth, and I valued integrity. As a result, this action of my father's really aggravated me. He was being dishonest even when he was very likely to win anyway – how unfair was that? So I did what came naturally – I called it out. I can't remember now whether I did so jovially or in great earnest or protest, but I was certainly not prepared for what happened next. To my logical brain, it was obvious that my father had cheated, so surely this was a safe time to shine a light on his actions since he wouldn't be able to sidestep it. How wrong I was.

The Thundercloud immediately appeared, and my father strongly refuted my claims. I was so outraged that I persisted. Things didn't go well. The game ended prematurely, but my father's anger carried on unabated. I assumed he would own up, as surely that was what an honest human being would do? But no – eventually he forced me to recant what I had said, to declare that I must have been mistaken. I remember distinctly feeling the throbbing burn of injustice and the ignominious stab of defeat as I withdrew the truth and spoke a falsehood. It made no sense: I was still absolutely rock solid in my understanding of what had happened. But I couldn't outgun my father's Thundercloud, so I had to give in to restore order to our household – at least as much for Mummy's sake as for my own, since it was obvious how much she hated family strife.

So the fight option wasn't really on the table for me. Running away was my primary, primal urge – to simply escape the shouting, the anger, the madness. To escape the parent who in that moment no longer made any sense to me, who didn't give me safe harbour, and who indeed actively scared me. But of course, a child isn't generally able to just run away like that. Whilst I would eventually be able to go to my room, that wasn't really far enough away – there was after all an oppressive Thundercloud hanging over the entire house. And I couldn't stay in my room forever. Added to which I tended to be in my father's presence when the Thundercloud emerged, and he wouldn't generally just let me leave straight away.

Of course, I did eventually flee – that memorable Christmas Eve at 11:30pm. But even then I wasn't allowed to flee for long, and what I believed to be a compassionate rescue after my father had come to his senses actually ended up feeling more like a recapturing. "Are you ready to give in yet, Alexandra?"

I also fought my father more as I grew older, as I developed more strength to counter him, more confidence in my abilities, and a greater sense of injustice at some of the things he would say. But such resistance used to result in more fireworks, so I had to be very clear what I was letting myself in for.

Back to younger Alexandra, who didn't really have the option to fight or flee. It turns out that, under such circumstances, the body reaches for two other options: freeze or fawn.

The freeze response is similar to a common animal response to throw off a predator: playing dead. Mice do it when chased by a cat, gazelles do it when chased by a cheetah, rabbits do it when chased by a fox. They can literally go limp while in the jaws of death. The Virginia opossum takes the whole concept a step further by also secreting a foul-smelling liquid. The hope is that the predator in question will lose interest and walk away.

These animals adopt a process officially called thanatosis, unconsciously adopting the freeze response and completely shutting down. They then magically come back to life after the predator leaves, and walk away pretty much unscathed from the scene of the crime.

Little Alexandra used to adopt a similar freeze approach – not quite playing dead, although wouldn't that be quite the party trick if one could pull it off? But she certainly used to shut down emotionally and physically, shrinking down as small as possible, and tried to say as little as possible to avoid stoking the fire. She would just wait out the storm and pray for calmer weather. Underneath, she would feel sick to the pit of her stomach, she would be cold and shaky, and she would wonder what horrible stuff she must have done to deserve this.

If she was directly in the line of fire and couldn't simply shut down, fawning was the next most obvious tactic. She would do anything she could to placate her father. She might try to be helpful in some way, in vain hopes of cheering him up. Or she might profess to agree with stuff she quite simply didn't agree with, to make him feel authoritative and avoid a fight. Or she might attempt to engage in a debate with her father even though she absolutely hated doing so, because he seemingly relished the tension of it all. But of course, she mustn't go too far and say what she really thought, if that was likely to cause an eruption – so there was a complex tightrope to be walked.

The effects on Adult Alexandra

Let's cast our minds back to my spellbinding dark comedy from earlier – the guy who is whacked by a mallet that materialises from thin air on his birthday, every year without fail. It messes with his head, but he works his way through the puzzle and eventually figures out what's going on and the mallet is defeated. He can get on with enjoying his birthdays now, right? Happily ever after and all that?

I used to believe that. I used to think that, as I grew older and understood more what was going on, I could just leave the difficult feelings behind. Even if the situation re-emerged, I could knuckle down and cope better as a well-equipped adult. It turns out that this was only half true. Yes, I could absolutely respond more tactically in the moment. And I was able to exert more power in the relationship with my father as I grew older, wiser and emotionally stronger, even if he made it pretty much impossible for me to ever win outright. But the feelings remained – prickling nerves, sickening dread, gnawing anxiety, and palpable fear, to name but a few. I just couldn't shake them off. And these feelings would spill over even when he wasn't around, infiltrating and colouring my entire life. I did not feel safe in any situation. Something could go wrong at any minute. I needed to be in a state of constant alert just to make sure that I was ready to respond.

Christmas remained important to me. Once married, I would try to make the most of Advent when I was at home with my husband, Simon. We would go to Christmas shows, eat festive meals in fancy restaurants, and spend fun time with family and friends. But Christmas itself was always complicated for me. Even if we spent it with Simon's family, I would tend to feel tense and find something or other very difficult. Family gatherings were particularly hard, and I might go very quiet in company or feel the need to get out for a walk. I would often get tetchy with Simon and struggle to keep it together. I wouldn't really understand why I was reacting that way, and I felt extremely ashamed for spoiling a special time for Simon and other family members.

I remember once, in a moment of searing honesty, letting my father know that I struggled with the memories of particularly tough family times. He replied simply that it was best not to dwell on such things. I can't fault the logic on one level – the trouble is, I discovered the hard way that suppression isn't an effective strategy.

Whilst it might be the fervent hope of every child who has suffered in some way that the imprint of traumatic experiences will just disappear when the problem goes away, unfortunately it doesn't seem to hold true. I suppose a cushion that has only been sat on once might generally bounce back, but if it is repeatedly sat on in the same way, it will develop a lasting dent...

No doubt you have picked up that the picture I have painted of family Christmases is part of a wider story. It wasn't just at Christmas that the Thundercloud appeared, Christmas was merely a concentrated microcosm of a wider situation. At the end of the day, the only way to get to the other side is to really go through the feelings and deal with what happened. A necessary first step for me was coming to the realisation that I was traumatised. Deeply so. That literally took years, but that's a story for another time.

By Christmas 2021, I had made a lot of headway on that delicate and complex journey which cannot be rushed. However, I was so deeply enmeshed in the process and in my cocktail of emotions that I could not even contemplate the festive season. Simon and I withdrew from Christmas completely. We visited no-one: not my father, so that he couldn't hurt me; but not anyone else either. We had no decorations in our house. I didn't play or sing any carols, or listen to any Christmas songs on the radio. And although we bought some turkey out of some kind of habit, we made no plans for when we would eat it. On Christmas Day itself, we went for a rather soggy but beautiful Scottish walk. Our Christmas lunch consisted of piping hot spiced soup from flasks next to a waterfall, and our unexpected gift was finding a grassy old road that we've loved ever since. It was rather wonderful in its way, and shielded me from harm for one Christmas, but it wasn't a lasting solution to the fundamental problem.

Since then, I have become estranged from my father – a story that I might be able to tell you about in more detail at another time. This was triggered by a seismic event that I was not expecting, and that I could not ignore. While in some ways it has been tragic to see this situation unfold, it has brought me considerable relief, if I'm being totally honest. Six months in as I write this account, I'm already happier, bolder, freer. I'm much more consistently able to be myself.

But now Christmas is in front of me again – 2022. Darn the unerring consistency of the calendar! It feels like a huge Mount Everest towering ominously ahead of me. I have realised that, although the estrangement means that there is no danger of the past repeating itself, the anxiety and stress about Christmas are hard-wired into me. I am habitually haunted by bad Christmas memories, by the malevolent ghosts of Christmas past. Even the mention of Christmas presents, or a short refrain from a much-loved carol, or the thought of putting up Christmas decorations, have been enough recently to make me cry bitter tears and want nothing more than to run away yet again.

I am currently totally unable to connect to the goodness that I have relished in the past. It feels completely unattainable. I am also terrified of trying to enjoy Christmas and failing again – if I mess it up, surely

I'll just make my problem even worse? Grown-up Alexandra is hamstrung by what little Alexandra went through. What used to light her up about Christmas now comes as a package deal with a goodly dose of dread, tears and heartache.

So where to go from here?

Part Two: The seeds of hope

In which I recognise that something deep inside me can't give up hope, and that I will need to go beyond logic to find my desired destination.

Chapter 4: Something in me can't give up

There's a light that shines more brightly than the darkness
Despite everything that has happened to spoil Christmas, something in me can't give up. Somewhere deep inside me, I know what beautiful looks like, and my soul longs achingly to get back to that place of beauty. It is emblematic of my strong, gut-led pull to heal from the wounds of my childhood. Although I have often felt totally consumed by the hurt, surrounded by darkness, held firmly in the quagmire, it has always been against my deeper will. Even when I just couldn't see a way out, I couldn't stop trying – even when my efforts felt extraordinarily feeble, I was still trying to take baby steps.

I think that must be a common human trait. I have read moving accounts by people who have managed to free themselves from past hurts. I have been particularly touched by some who write as healthcare professionals, for whom that process of finding freedom from their own pain augmented their book-learning to further human knowledge of how to help those in need.

I have a passionate desire to focus on the light, the flame that ushers me forward to a happier life, despite the chains that keep me bound in the painful here and now. However dim it might appear at times, however at risk the flame might seem to be of being snuffed out, I keep searching for it, wanting to get closer to its reassuring glow.

I long to help the flame burn more brightly, so that it cannot be blown out by the winds of pain, sorrow and toxic memories.

Fundamentally, I long for the light to outshine the darkness. And at my core, I believe that it can.

I have always been drawn to stories of people overcoming huge, seemingly insurmountable obstacles. A frail human being managing to reach beyond their weakness and take hold of a deeper truth, a new life, a shining hope. I literally cry my eyes out at books or films like this.

A Beautiful Mind is one of those films. It's based on the story of John Nash, a mathematical genius who was on the brink of an incredible discovery early on in his career. Then complex mental health issues rampaged through this life. Again, without giving away too much of the plot in case you are inspired to go and watch it, he eventually managed to overcome ugly odds and won the Nobel Memorial Prize in Economic Sciences. More importantly than that for me, he was portrayed as being at peace with his demons at the end of the film. I was a sobbing wreck as I watched his ups and downs and saw him finally triumph. There were no trumpet fanfares, no arrogant displays of victory, but simply a quiet affirmation that he had made it to a long-desired destination of calm and equanimity in his soul.

I want to be one of those people who manages to overcome. Who is at peace, who feels joy consistently in their life.

So, what does this look like for my relationship with Christmas? I think it boils down to the strong conviction that my father doesn't have the right to ruin things for me – not Christmas, and not anything else. This is not about being angry – although I will freely admit that, as I have become more aware of the truth, I have been full of rage at what he has done to me. But I am moving beyond that anger, recognising that I will never know how much he has done these things consciously and how much unconsciously. What I do know is that he is a flawed human being, as all of us are, and it will not serve me to hold onto anger about what he inflicted on me. Beyond anger, I am now ready to state this truth, that he doesn't get to have the last word in my life.

Ironically, my father sometimes mentioned a phrase when I was finding things hard that has stuck with me: journey hopefully. That is what I feel compelled to do each day, even when I do not appear to be very hopeful. I want to journey hopefully back to the light that stubbornly, gloriously and miraculously will not go out.

What do I really believe?

I nearly didn't write this section for fear of putting you off the rest of the book. Faith and belief: big words, and often hotly contested. But the reason that I felt compelled to write this section is because of something I hold to be deeply true, that what you believe about yourself and the world will affect how you live your life, including when the inevitable trials and tribulations appear.

This is because the stuff we tell ourselves each day – our guiding principles and that endless inner chatter that can seem almost impossible to silence – guides how our brain sees and operates in the world. It is like the inputs or parameters given to a computer, which guide how it runs its programs.

I am not seeking to compare one world view or belief system to another, but rather to explore the role in healing of core aspects of faith and belief that can be found in all of us. Some of us have inherited faith and beliefs, some of us have discovered and adopted them, and some of us don't call them anything quite so formal. But we all have them in some form or other, whether consciously or unconsciously. And yet, for topics that are common to all of us, faith and belief are not discussed much.

For my own part, I have grown up in a culture where we are taught to respect each other's beliefs, but not necessarily to talk about them.

I think that discussion about differing beliefs is often considered to be too dangerous, like a stick of dynamite that is best left untouched. This means that there is not much opportunity to stretch our perceptions and understanding together, to question our faiths, to dive into our beliefs.

And within groups that share a belief, there tends to be an assumption that 'one size fits all', and so there is limited discussion of things that some of us within a group find challenging. And of course, many people have beliefs, but not as part of a particular group, which I imagine is liberating for some but might be isolating for others.

So, it seems that we are often pretty much left to sort out our own beliefs by ourselves, or perhaps with some close friends with whom we have built up sufficient trust. I think we are missing a trick here by not feeling safe to talk about our beliefs and explore the mysteries of the universe and human existence together. I wish that I could learn more from other people, whether their beliefs are similar or different to mine.

You might have a clear view of what you believe. Or you may not have spent much time thinking about this, and are subconsciously floating down a river perhaps without realising which river you are on or how the journey might unfold.

I will tell you a bit about my core beliefs, not because I'm trying to convert you to my way of seeing the world, but simply to illustrate how my healing journey was impacted by my beliefs.

Firstly, I now realise that for a long time I believed that my father had ultimate power over me, and that I didn't have any choice about that. It turns out that was a faulty belief: we always have choices, but only if we believe that we have choices will we look for alternatives to the painful status quo.

In the end, the relationship with my father had to come to an end. A line was crossed, one that experts had advised me was definitive, and I simply couldn't see another viable alternative that would allow me to be safe, let alone content and fulfilled. That was a deeply tragic truth to acknowledge, but it was the moment when I finally rejected the old beliefs that he had the power and that I had no choice, and fully embraced the true and healthy belief that I had choices. I do not regret what happened: it is undeniable to those who know me the best that I have grown immeasurably more in the period since the estrangement than I ever managed to achieve before.

Secondly, I'm a Christian who believes in God – but mine is a faith that has had quite a few twists and turns as I have tried to make sense of the world and my predicament, almost to the point where I wondered if I might lose my faith altogether.

I started off with a fairly light touch Christian upbringing – I knew the main Bible stories, I sang hymns at school, and I went to church at Christmas. It was when I went to university that my personal faith blossomed. I found myself part of a community of students whose devotion and kind, dedicated way of living fundamentally attracted me. Even people who didn't naturally get on with each other so well made efforts to love and support each other. It felt very new and special to me, an appealing alternative to my family life. I lapped up the joy of belonging to such a loving group, and I spent a lot of time listening to the teachings of various ministers and chaplains.

The problem came when I began to question some of what I was being taught, and the incongruence with the central tenet of compassion and kindness that was so important for me. I wondered if that meant my whole faith would unravel. But I couldn't stop myself from asking those questions, no matter where they led me. Why were women not allowed to take up certain roles in most churches, and why should they submit to their husbands in marriage? In whatever way Christians presented these issues, the explanations just didn't make sense to me. And why would the church disapprove of gay unions when there is no record of Jesus making any proclamation on this topic? After all, love is love, and faithfulness is faithfulness – so why, in the face of so much darkness and suffering in the world, would we want to limit the amount of true love and faithfulness in the world by placing limits on who can participate? And on a personal level, was it really true that God would never let you be tested more than you could cope with? I wasn't at all sure about that one. I saw terrible things happening to people all the time, and I witnessed terrible things happening to me. The questions just kept coming.

I slowly found my way through these struggles to a more liberal faith. I was greatly encouraged to find that there were many other people making a similar journey, seeking to deconstruct the faith that had been handed to them as a package deal of inalienable truth, and to rebuild it into something that they could actually feel firmly rooted in and stand behind in their everyday lives. This resonated with me so strongly, because it is all about whether or not we feel congruence in our minds and souls – if we try to believe something that just doesn't fit with our key values and tenets of how we see the world, we will feel a strong dis-ease in our system that we won't be able to shift.

Overall, it could have been a lot easier for me just to give up my faith in the face of all my questions. But I found that I couldn't give up on the core of my beliefs, the idea of a good God. I have a fundamental yearning in my soul for a true light that simply cannot be found within the ranks of human beings. With my faith, I can see glimpses and reflections of that light every day. And I need someone who stands up for those in need and against those in the wrong. Jesus stood up for the poor and powerless, wreaking havoc amongst the religious elite of his day with his radical shake-ups of established teachings. I came to the view that the radical example of Jesus has been reduced to certainty and rules by many churches and denominations – because fundamentally people feel more comfortable with clear-cut rules by which to live. This makes them feel safer because they know where they stand, things are reassuringly black and white. But I think the truth is far scarier, but also more liberating. The only real "rules" I believe in are to love God, and to love others as you love yourself. There are so many layers within those statements which I think sum up faith in a nutshell.

So, during this process, which took a number of years, something deep inside of me held onto the concept of a good God. And by the way, I don't picture "God" as a wise old man nowadays, I now think he/she/it is so much more awesome, unfathomable, and beyond our capacity as humans to truly dream or imagine. I think we will have our breath taken away when we see the truth!

It is this belief that has kept me searching for the light, even when darkness has threatened to drown me.

For some Christians, this hope is about the Biblical promise of life after death. But to be honest, I'm less concerned with what happens after I die, and more preoccupied with making the most of my current life. Not in a greedy, trampling sort of way, believing that I am more important than anyone else so I can grasp for whatever I want no matter the consequences for other people or the natural world. But rather, I want to make the very best of the hand I've been dealt in this life. I want to look back on my life as I'm dying and be really satisfied with how I chose to live, and how I did my very best to prevail despite the huge monsters that came along to terrify and derail me.

I want to run the best race I can run, armed with the belief that a benevolent higher power that we choose to call God is all around me and helping me. Not just handing things to me on a platter, but there to guide in intangible ways if I'm open to them.

What do you really believe?

I'm not sharing my belief journey because I want to convince you to believe what I do. I'm sharing it in the hope that, if you haven't thought much about your beliefs, seeing an example might encourage you to think about them some more. I also think we can be too nervous to share our belief stories for fear of being ridiculed or told that we are wrong – which means that we don't engage as much as we could in the mystery in which we find ourselves here on Planet Earth.

Am I right in my beliefs? I honestly don't know, and I don't know how anyone could know for sure. I have genuinely wrestled with my beliefs and come to a point where my faith has withstood the rigours of much prodding and probing, with some evolution along the way. I have been honest about what I believe. I trust that God will be gentle with those who have followed the calling of their souls in love, even if they stray from a particular truth in some way – and I'm open to the idea that that could include me.

But the whole point of thinking about faith in this book is that I really do believe that what you believe matters. Your beliefs are like an unseen satnav system which guides the direction you are going in, and affects your perceptions of what is possible and impossible in this life.

You may be very sure of your beliefs and why you believe them. On the other hand, you may be less sure – in which case I would really encourage you to devote some time to pondering this big question. You may be sure about what you do not believe – what you are against – but may have less clarity about what you believe – what you are for.

We live in a profoundly mysterious world with questions that have preoccupied human beings for millennia, for as long as we have had the brains capable of thinking through these sorts of questions. Do you think there is reason or purpose behind this universe and our place in it? If so, what is that purpose? If not, where does that conclusion lead you?

Overall, it's important to know what you believe about life, the universe and everything. This is not just about logic, but about what you feel to be true deep inside yourself – that guiding voice that can often be drowned out by the busyness of the world, by our worries and preoccupations, by the endless demands that others make of us.

What you believe will shape how you see the world around you, and how you will shape that world. So please take the time to listen to that inner voice, and reach out to people you trust. And try not to be overly defensive – question yourself, test what you think you believe, and expose yourself to a range of thinking and ideas. That way, when you have beliefs that guide you, they will be firmly rooted and not easily swayed or broken by the trials and tribulations of life.

Chapter 5: I can't think my way out of this one

The primacy of logic

I don't know about you, but I was raised to believe in the majesty and superiority of the human brain. Implicit in my upbringing was the tenet that we should be able to reason our way out of every conundrum, since logic is the ultimate tool that we have at our disposal to crack every problematic nut.

I was a bright kid, so this should be even more the case for me, right? I could learn pretty much anything I put my mind to, and this features in one of my stronger childhood memories.

My father had taught me Pythagoras' theorem by rote on his knee as a young child: "The area of the square of the hypotenuse is equal to the sum of the areas of the squares of the other two sides." I had literally no idea what that sentence meant – no one told me it was about triangles or explained what a hypotenuse was, for a start! But then came the magical moment in class aged about twelve when our maths teacher gave us some triangles to investigate, to see if we could discern a pattern. She obviously expected this task to take up the entire lesson. Suddenly, my neurons started firing and making a set of deductions like dominos falling. Within about five minutes, I stuck my hand excitedly up in the air to tell my teacher I had figured out the answer. To say that she was gobsmacked is a considerable understatement.

Then there was the time in a science class when we were going through GCSE papers and I knew the teacher was giving everyone the wrong answer. I was confident enough in my cognitive abilities to pipe up and have a debate with her in front of the whole class. I think my willingness to confront the situation came from a desire that my classmates not be misled and therefore disadvantaged in the upcoming exams. It was excruciating though, and I lived with the negative consequences of that intervention for some time.

Mathematics became my enduring best friend – I understood its foundational concepts and clear language, and most importantly, I could depend on it. There was always a correct answer. No debates, complications, or what ifs – just a correct answer. It was clear-cut, built solely on logic, with no space for different opinions or interpretations.

By contrast, I had no time for the subject of English literature – while I adored reading and insatiably devoured books as a youngster, the idea of dissecting a text to probe different potential meanings and motivations filled me with dread. And history was another bugbear – we had incomplete bits of imperfect evidence and had to deduce what reality might have looked like from that evidence. And of course, again there were myriad areas of interpretation and ambiguity.

Looking back, I think I found the chaos and uncertainty of our world deeply unsettling, and the realm of mathematics gave me an anchor where I could be sure of how things would unfold if I just applied clear, unassailable logic. Why couldn't all of the world be as predictable as that?

Our human capacity for logical reasoning is an important key to our success as a species. Our larger brains with the newer, more recently evolved neocortex designed for logical reasoning have enabled us to achieve things that would have seemed totally unthinkable and magical to our ancestors: flying through the air in a massive metal box, landing on the moon, creating lifelike images on a flat screen, and healing a whole host of life-threatening diseases, to name just a few mind-blowing examples.

I used to think of my brain as a single unit, a unified computer that I could use and direct pretty much at will to solve the problems that came my way. However, the truth is far more complex. It amazes me that we are given this awesomely complex machine at birth – the most complex object in the known universe in fact – and yet are never really taught how it works or how to use it properly. Now of course in the past, no one knew how it functioned – and even though much remains mysterious even today, there is so much more understanding which can help us to function better in the world.

One simplified model of the brain which, while it may have its deficiencies, can help us to get a basic grip on what is happening in our very own personal computers, is that of the triune brain, a model formulated by neuroscientist Paul D MacLean in the 1960s. As well as the logical, most recent addition of the neocortex for logical reasoning, there are two other parts. The reptilian brain is the oldest, most primitive part, responsible for basic survival functions such as heart rate, breathing and temperature. It will take over if survival is threatened, overruling higher parts of the brain if needs be. Then there is the limbic system.

We are actually profoundly emotional beings

The limbic system has been coined our "emotional brain". In fact, though we may pride ourselves on being fundamentally logical creatures, the bald truth is that we are not – we are in fact ruled by our emotions far more than we like to believe. The limbic system is responsible for the stress responses I outlined in Chapter 3 – fight, flight, freeze and fawn. But it goes much broader and deeper than that – the limbic system fundamentally shapes how we experience the world. It subconsciously filters our experiences and determines whether we need to remember them, and in what state of mind. For example, when we have a scary experience, it will be filed away in our memories and the limbic system will essentially add a label marked 'fear'. And in future when we encounter a similar situation, or even just think about the original memory, the limbic system will read the label and we will feel the fear. It's very circular and self-reinforcing.

While I may have been famous at school for my intelligence, I was also well known for the strength of my emotions. When I was about seven, my teachers confided in my parents that they were concerned about me because I would often cry at school, perhaps even as frequently as every day. I know they meant well in doing this, but this intervention unleashed something that they could not have anticipated, something that did nothing to resolve the so-called problem and in fact considerably aggravated it. My father instigated the "Toughen Alexandra up" campaign. "You need to become thicker skinned," he used to say as he challenged me to yet another stressful debate at the dinner table to see if I could hold my own more confidently than during the last bruising bout.

Of course, the debate wasn't stressful to him – he loved the verbal parrying and the back and forth of points and counter-points. This was his bread and butter. But I hated it – partly because I had an allergic reaction to conflict, and partly because this could never be described as an equal contest. And of course, because I knew from experience that there was the risk that I might inadvertently say the 'wrong thing' and cause the Thundercloud to appear. So the stakes always felt very high during "Toughen Alexandra up" lessons.

I am genuinely sure that my father meant well in these endeavours. His parents will have taught him to keep his emotions in check, as was the norm at the time. Emotions were believed to be unhelpful, since they got in the way of achieving what was counted as success. The British stiff upper lip, and all that.

And it didn't stop with school. My father will have been taught that being emotional was simply not something you did at work. I remember when he told me I must never be seen to cry at work. If I felt tears bubbling to the surface, I must go to the bathroom and pull myself together before I let anyone see me again. I would never get ahead if people thought I was emotional, flaky and easily thrown. I wondered why it was considered acceptable for men to be emotional in the form of anger in the workplace, but not for women to show that they were upset? I realise that's a gender generalisation, but it is often how emotions play out in the office. Male aggression is all too easily excused as thrusting purposefully towards a goal and overcoming obstacles, while women being upset is often thought of as out of place, embarrassing other people and distracting them from their true purpose. Looking back, it was particularly ironic for my father to condemn me being upset when those emotions were largely elicited by his emotions of aggression.

So, from a young age and through to my early adulthood, I tried to learn to be someone I am not – a robot that did what was needed with the minimum of fuss and unnecessary emotional turbulence. The problem was that this wasn't the true, whole me – it was only part of me, and the other, suppressed part of me was frustrated, misunderstood, and struggling to get out.

As hard as I tried, the emotions kept surfacing and, worse than that, I began to develop mental health conditions, which multiplied as time went on. I have had a phobia of spiders for as long as I can remember – a really, really debilitating fear that my friends and colleagues would find intriguing and think was a bit over the top. Then when I was a teenager, I developed an exaggerated fear of germs, which I would later learn was a version of obsessive compulsive disorder (OCD). OCD comes in many forms, and it flared up afresh in my late twenties with another twist: a grave fear of affecting others badly and irretrievably via my actions or inactions.

The challenges became all-consuming and frightening. The pile-up of strong emotions and powerful fears led me to believe that my brain was fundamentally flawed. While I tried to reason my way out of these issues, that invariably didn't work. Someone who had once thought she could rely on her brain began to be convinced that it was badly programmed and that there was nothing she could do about it.

It would be years before someone would explain the concept of the highly sensitive person to me, a concept that is backed up by scientific evidence. Up to one in five of the population – one in five! – experience the world in greater technicolour than the rest, ascending to loftier highs and diving to deeper lows as they ride the waves of their more expansive emotions. As I first learned about this concept, I characteristically wept – but these were tears of joy. Tears of feeling understood and accepted. Tears of realising that I wasn't alone. Tears of finally recognising that there wasn't something fundamentally wrong with me. I was beautifully made, I was simply made differently to the majority of the population, and counter to the prevailing culture and norms.

I have come to the realisation that, rather than being a problem as my father made me believe, having high sensitivity has bestowed great gifts on me. The ability to empathise tenderly with others and almost tangibly feel what they are going through. The ability to feel the glorious gamut of life's experiences with much greater depth and vitality than many do. That means experiencing the good stuff more vividly, but also of course the bad and the ugly stuff more harshly. Over time, however, I came to see that even that downside contained a gift. I could really, really feel my emotions – and human emotions are actually vitally important signposts to what is going on with us. We can choose to ignore them, or we can choose to explore them and unearth the story beneath them, which is in the end the only way that I believe we will truly heal from life's hurts. Awareness of our emotions is a key starting point, and many people don't really begin this journey.

And my high sensitivity had generously given me another gift: the gift of creativity. My emotions were more readily acceptable to people when expressed through creative outlets. I was gifted at music, quickly progressing through the exam grades after starting to play the piano aged seven. I can't remember when I began composing music. I'm no Mozart, but I found I could put together memorable melodies with some Alexandra-shaped twists that grew and developed as I did.

This culminated in the composition of a musical at university, based on the book of Esther in the Old Testament of the Bible. It's perfect ready-made musical fodder – with goodies, baddies, love, betrayal, and a whole range of human emotions at play. And of course, plenty of obstacles for the goodies to overcome before the eventual happy ending. I wrote the guts of the musical in ten days – ten days! – while I was working on a project in the maths department during the summer holidays.

If someone were to ask me where this composing ability comes from or how I do it, I couldn't begin to explain. It is as simple and as complicated as sitting down at the piano, experimenting with fragments of tunes and lyrics that come into my head, and letting the magic unfurl. Of course, my super-charged ability to feel and express emotions has to be a key ingredient in this process.

Interestingly, when I was younger, I firmly believed that I was hopeless at art. A particular low point that sticks in my memory was when we were asked to create "night and day" pictures – a scene where one half was depicted in daylight and the other half in darkness. I was rather proud of my finished product of a natural landscape complete with animals appropriate to day-time and night-time. Then one of my good friends came over to have a look, and innocently asked why there were watering cans in the foreground of the night-time part. They weren't watering cans, I sadly explained, they were badgers...!

As a result of such misadventures, I had written myself off as an artist. But my senior school art teacher saw potential in me that I had not recognised, and was determined to light the spark. She endlessly encouraged me, and actually persuaded me to take Art and Design GCSE a year early, since I had already picked a full range of subjects and that was the only way I would have space to include art. She slowly built up my belief and drew out what was inside of me, and I ended up achieving the highest grade at GCSE. Not only that, but I continued to pursue art at A-Level. I reasoned with my parents that it would give me light relief alongside the intellectually hefty mixture of mathematics and science. I also achieved the highest grade in A-Level Art, something that would have seemed to me to be fundamentally impossible – in fact totally laughable – just a few years earlier.

Our body – simply a vehicle for travelling through this world?

When I ponder how I have viewed my body over the years, I have had the usual hang-ups about how I look and how attractive I am. But fundamentally, it seems that I have viewed my body rather like a machine that needs to operate in order for me to function in life. A bit like a car really – I expect it to move me from A to B and perform various basic functions, and I get really frustrated when it stops working. It's just supposed to work, darn it!

I have been pretty lucky with my body over the years so far. No broken bones, no chronic physical conditions, and only one major life-threatening illness. But nonetheless some serious niggles that have held me back. Notably, troubled sleep starting in childhood and becoming a complete lack of ability to sleep properly since early adulthood. Now obviously there is a strong mental component to sleep and insomnia – in my case, I think that a fundamental sense of unease was often at the root. But in adulthood I have also experienced my insomnia as a problem with physical causes and symptoms. For example, the agony of never-ending backache played a big part in entrenching my sleeping problems, no doubt in a vicious cycle. And there was the sheer physical exhaustion of having to try to function on as little as two hours' sleep, day in day out, for years on end. There was a deep irony in being wide awake in the middle of the night and then having a major fight with myself to crawl out of bed for work when the alarm inevitably went off.

I threw all the logic I could at my sleeping problem. My thinking brain attacked the issue from every angle it could rustle up. And, to be fair, that made a tangible improvement. When travelling and sleeping on strange beds, I discovered that if I carried a duvet around with me wherever I went, I could soften most hard mattresses enough to not be in intolerable discomfort. I followed all the sleep hygiene techniques you could imagine: a white noise machine, specialist earplugs, a plush eye mask, thick bedroom curtains, and no stressful or stimulating activities like TV watching or phone scrolling in the bedroom. And if I found myself lying awake for more than about fifteen minutes, I would dutifully get up and do something non-stressful in another room until I felt sleepy again. The problem was, no matter how hard I tried, I would tend to be wide awake for about three hours. Which gouges a gaping hole in one's sleep timetable.

Physical exercise proved to be absolutely vital to stabilise my sleeping regime – up to a point. Certainly, I figured out that things deteriorated quickly if I didn't get exercise. I became a rather avid fan of certain celebrity exercise videos in my late twenties, which introduced me to the wonderful positive feelings caused by endorphin release when we move our bodies around.

I even participated in a cognitive behavioural technique called sleep restriction therapy. At its heart was the notion that perhaps we insomniacs were trying to sleep for too long, and actually we needed to let go of the magic eight hours obsession, and train ourselves to sleep well for a shorter period of time that was better suited to our specific needs. It is a pretty scientific method – starting from how much sleep you reckon you get on average, you only allow yourself to stay in bed for that amount of time, tops. So, if you estimate you have been sleeping for five and a half hours a night, you would go to bed at, say, midnight, and get up at 5:30am, no matter how much shut-eye you had actually managed to snatch. (If your average sleep time is really low, you wouldn't go below a base time period of around five hours.) Without religiously clock-watching, which in itself can bring about anxiety that prevents good sleep, you would note down roughly how much sleep you believed you had achieved each night. Only when you were consistently sleeping for 90% of the allotted time would you be allowed to increase your sleep window, by fifteen minutes. And so, the process would continue until you reached an equilibrium time, where you weren't able to consistently sleep for longer.

All of this worked, but only up to a point. By sticking to these techniques, I could get into a pattern of achieving a respectable amount of sleep most nights of the week. There were always glitches, particularly on Sunday nights when I generally wasn't looking forward to work... But even that pattern was tenuous and vulnerable to disruption by pressures and stresses – so I would often have to reset my sleep pattern by going through painful sleep restriction again. My sleep pattern is still pretty shocking by most people's standards. I try not to worry about all the research that talks about the dastardly impact of sleep deprivation on one's overall health. After all, that is only going to make my anxiety – and my sleep – worse.

I would become frustrated at my body for not being able to function just the way I needed it to in order to achieve my goals. Particularly if I got injured in some way and wasn't able to exercise for a while, I would almost take it as a personal slight. After all, when a car goes wrong you can just take it into the garage and it will generally emerge as good as new in a day or two. But with a human injury, it can take weeks. Weeks of patience and resting, which I found anything but restful!

So, at best I saw my body as a means to an end – achieving what I wanted to achieve in life – and at worst, which became more and more frequent over time, I viewed it as something that actively got in the way of achieving my goals.

Deep down, I knew that there were bigger underlying reasons for my chronic insomnia – particularly the fact that I just didn't feel safe or comfortable in the world. How could I possibly relax in a world where such terrible things happen on a regular basis? And yet other people could know about those same terrible things and be very sad about them, and even want to change them, but be able to relax in their own circumstances. So, what was so different about me?

Some modern trauma researchers have focused on the impact of trauma on the body. It turns out that, even when the trauma is over and one is technically safe – and indeed the mind can acknowledge logically that one is safe – the body holds the imprint of what has happened, and isn't easily able to let go of or change that imprint.

Let's go back to that concept of animals playing dead to avoid being captured by a predator. If the predator does indeed get bored and go away, the prey can emerge as if by magic from its frozen state and carry on as if nothing has happened. It may shake itself off a bit as it does so.

In humans, when our limbic system primes us to fight or flee in the presence of danger, a huge amount of energy is made available to us to initiate either of those responses as required. We have all heard stories of parents who have summoned up seemingly unbelievable strength to rescue their child from a perilous situation. And anyone who has run away from something frightening would attest to the fact that they were able to run faster and for longer than would normally be possible for them.

But sometimes, our lizard brain realises that fighting or fleeing are both losing bets, and catapults us into temporary immobility. It has been suggested that, in this situation, the large doses of energy are still there, but aren't being used for anything. If that energy isn't discharged in some way, we hang onto it – perhaps we aren't able to let go of it, or perhaps we are scared or embarrassed of the consequences of letting that energy out in potentially irrational and uncontrolled ways. But the problem is that this stuck energy impacts our bodies in a range of ways that prevent us from moving forward and living a full life.

Another way of looking at it is that the body hangs onto past stress. It doesn't know that the trauma is over and won't be repeated. It is anticipating danger like a coiled spring, ready to jump into damage limitation mode at the slightest provocation. Think about all the pent-up stress from repeated negative experiences over the years – when I came across this theory, it seemed obvious to me why I was inherently less relaxed than my fellow human beings. Stress would obviously manifest itself in tight muscles, aches and pains, stiffness and soreness.

In fact, researchers believe that trauma has negative impacts on the body that can lead to all sorts of chronic health conditions. These physical conditions are another layer of baggage from our past troubles that hold us back in life. In some ways I count myself lucky that I haven't experienced worse bodily symptoms...

Modern somatic therapy focuses on how we feel our emotions through our body. We may think of our emotions as originating in our mind, but actually, if we pay attention, we can normally associate those emotions with a bodily sensation. For me, stress normally conveys itself as a tension in my belly, and seeing something disturbing can elicit a tingle in my lower back.

If we can get more in touch with how our emotions manifest in our body, we can use these physical clues to see more clearly which emotions are bubbling up, including perhaps some that we haven't consciously recognised.

Moreover, we can then use physical responses associated with positive emotions for our benefit. As we recognise physical sensations that we associate with safety, we can develop more of a sense of 'bodily safety'. Think about what you feel in your body when you feel safe. Perhaps you feel a warm glow in your core, or perhaps you have a sense of being hugged by someone special.

The more we get into the habit of connecting with a physical sensation of safety, we can use that as an anchor to release our past stresses and meet our current life with greater equanimity. It will take time, but we can train our bodies to feel safer to put past challenges firmly behind us, and meet current challenges from a place of greater faith in our ability to rise to them. Until our body catches up with our mind, we may be caught in a stress and pain loop that frustrates our progress.

So, having spent years viewing my body as an inconvenient and sometimes unreliable means to an end, I'm now coming to see it as an intrinsic part of who I am, and a part that I should listen to really carefully to understand where I'm really at in life, and how to progress to a better, healthier future.

The enigma of the spirit

For me, there is a spiritual element to human beings which, if ignored, may frustrate our best efforts to heal from more complex issues.

Take my insomnia, which I always felt emanated from my deep dis-ease in a scary world where humans could not be relied upon to be good, helpful and honest. Coupled with that, I have always had a pretty unshakeable conviction that there is a profoundly good Higher Power at play in the universe. But nonetheless, said Higher Power had allowed a bunch of horrible stuff to happen to me at the hands of less scrupulous human beings. So, what was the Higher Power doing, and why wasn't he/she/it protecting me properly?

This conundrum left me with a profound lack of a sense of safety – if the Higher Power had let bad things happen to me before, then why not another time? When would that happen, and how? There was no way for me to know, and therefore the logical conclusion was for me to be constantly on edge, waiting for the next damaging blow.

My options here were fairly limited: accept the status quo, give up my belief in a Higher Power, or find some middle ground where there was a positive outcome after the hardship. Neither of the first two options were particularly appealing to me, which only left the final one.

Most religions have long wrestled with the problem of suffering in the presence of an omnipotent God. Many answers I heard to this conundrum felt contrived or forced. But I also knew that I had seen many people grow through adversity to achieve bigger and shinier things. Whilst it had always annoyed me hugely when my Christian counsellor explained that the only choice I had was in how to respond to events, I had to grudgingly admit that she had a point – I could either choose to let negative events drag me down, or I could grow through them and extract and absorb whatever learning they had to offer.

Which brings me back to the vexed question of Christmas. Rather than continuing to limp on through a seasonal celebration that will come around perennially whether I like it or not, perhaps I should look to see what opportunity there is to grow here, to find out more about myself and reclaim the joy of Christmas in my own special way...

Chapter 6: Designing my own rituals

The only way is through it

The only way for me to reclaim Christmas is to find a way through my current predicament. Last year I just sat it out – and that was the best choice for that moment in time, effectively a freeze response in order to survive. But I want to do more than simply ignore or survive the rest of the Christmases that I am blessed with here on earth – I want to recapture the joy. And if I want that, I need to go through the difficulties that are currently in front of me. Scary though that may be, it is perhaps less frightening than the concept of just sitting by the river's edge, too nervous to wade in and clamber over to the delights awaiting me at the other side.

No one wants to go through difficult, dark times, but sometimes there is no better option. These times can feel totally impenetrable, but there is no way out except getting to the other side. And no one else can get there on our behalf, we have to make the journey ourselves.

It has taken me a long time to fully appreciate that courage is not the absence of fear – courage is acting despite the gnawing, churning anxiety in the pit of your stomach. If you don't feel fear, you're not really being courageous. As a result of this insight, I now think it is weird that we think of courage as a key attribute of a lion. Isn't it remarkably easy to be brave when you are the most effective predator in your territory, the veritable King of the Jungle? Isn't it braver for an antelope to show up for life day after day, even if it instinctively senses the lurking presence of said lion?

I know that I need courage to face the journey ahead, and that I will encounter situations and feelings which will be distressing or at least deeply uncomfortable. I'm scared of messing things up still further, and becoming more injured in the process. What if I have another awful Christmas and then it really is doomed forever? I then quietly remind myself that nothing is irredeemable in this life if we have a will to see it through.

I'm actually more scared of never fully appreciating the joy of Christmas again. Therefore, I must journey onwards...

The alchemy of healing from trauma

There are many illnesses where the wonder of modern medicine has created a pretty much guaranteed solution. A vaccine to ward off what would otherwise be a life-threatening disease, antibiotics to clear up a bacterial infection, or an operation to remove an appendix where appendicitis has suddenly and painfully flared up.

Then there are cases where there are potential solutions but their efficacy varies from case to case. Some cancer treatments now have unbelievably consistent positive outcomes, whereas other cancer types remain more elusive and harder to treat. There may be a percentage chance of a positive outcome from chemotherapy, for example, depending on the patient's specific diagnosis. It is then up to them to decide whether they want to pursue that percentage chance of success, weighing up whether the potential benefits outweigh the known risks.

When it comes to the matter of healing from my childhood trauma and associated side effects, I have come to see the process as more alchemy than science. Alchemy was an early form of chemistry in the

Middle Ages aiming to turn common metals into gold. Although it is clear why that would be an attractive objective, our modern understanding of the periodic table tells us that alchemists were doomed to failure. Derived from that context, we now use the word alchemy in a slightly different way: to describe something that works so well that it looks like magic. Now, I'm not saying that I need magic to heal, but the combination of factors from which I have benefited over time, and the way in which the process has worked itself through me, have often felt more like a meandering journey of trial and error than a clear-cut scientific solution. I have felt gently led along a pathway to healing, in a way that could be encouraged but could not be rushed. I have partly been led by my wise counsellor who has journeyed alongside me for about fifteen years now, and partly by my own spirit seeking out answers.

There are a range of trauma healing methods out there nowadays, which each have their own take on how to untie the tight knot of trauma. I have come to the conclusion that I need to use my wisdom in whether and how to apply these in my particular context. Wise guides can give me their advice, but only I can really know what it is like to be me and to have experienced what I have experienced. Just as my insomnia wasn't completely fixed using a cognitive behavioural approach, similarly I believe in my case that the remedy for my trauma needs to work across my thinking mind, my emotional mind, my body, and my spirit.

I have heard healing described in this context as making sure that the environment is right, which then allows the internal healing work to happen naturally. This is analogous to what you do when you get a cut – you don't think that you have to heal it yourself somehow, but you make sure that the cut is clean and protected, and the body naturally follows the healing process as it is wired to do.

So how do we create the right environment for a more complex healing process? It is likely to take time, and it is important to figure out what works for you – which might be different to what works for other people, and might even surprise you. And once you've found what works, the key is to continue with those practices consistently – just as you would water a seed regularly to enable it to germinate and flourish.

The power of habits and rituals

I have long been fascinated by how we human beings think we are making conscious, rational choices all the time, but actually a lot of what we do is governed by habits that we formed subconsciously long ago. Some estimates suggest that around 40% of our daily actions are habitual. Now I don't know about you, but I find that somewhat unsettling since, whilst some of those habits are likely to be positive ones, I'm confident that many others will be less good for me. For example, I'm glad that I have a pretty consistent toothbrushing routine, but I'm less satisfied that I regularly give in to my chocolate cravings.

Habits are essentially mental short-cuts, to save our conscious minds from the exhausting prospect of having to make every single decision from scratch. Habits are driven by a neurological feedback loop whereby a cue of some sort sets off a craving, which leads to a response that delivers a reward. Over time, the brain associates the reward with the cue, and hence the loop is complete. In the case of my over-reliance on chocolate, the cue is generally that I want to feel good, leading to a craving – on a conscious level, I'm thinking about the particular taste and how good it feels to eat chocolate, but deeper down my brain is anticipating a hit of happy chemicals. More often than not, I eat some chocolate and am rewarded with the release of some warm and fuzzy neurochemicals that make me feel great, at least for a time.

At their best, habits help us to achieve amazing things – for example through a discipline of doing all the things that need to be done to achieve a purpose we desire, even if we don't feel like it every day. At their worst, habits can turn into addictions that sap people of their life energy and self-worth.

Now you might be wondering why our brains have evolved to create habits, since they seem to be a bit hit and miss in terms of whether they help or harm us. The reason is necessity – our conscious mind can only really focus on one thing at a time, much though we love to believe that we can multi-task. So, when the brain figures out through a process of trial and error that an issue can be solved in a particular way, that solution becomes coded into our unconscious mind, so that our conscious brain can focus on something more worthy of its undivided attention. Think about driving a car, for example. If you had to think consciously about every single action – from indicating, to depressing the accelerator, to turning the steering wheel – it would be a mind-frazzling task. (I'm thinking back to the trials and tribulations of my first driving lesson...!) But much of what you need to do becomes encoded in your brain and happens naturally, without you having to think about it. In fact, if you do try to intervene and think about what you are doing, you can end up thoroughly confusing yourself!

There is a habit that I realise I have picked up from my childhood experiences: learned helplessness. Because I had found that, time and time again, I couldn't change the outcome and the Thundercloud appeared regardless, I stopped trying to improve my circumstances. While I have always had a drive to heal, equally there have often been times where I have thrown my hands up in the air theatrically and declared something to be impossible to fix.

The good news is that habits can be changed. While we used to believe that the adult human brain was set in stone having developed during childhood and adolescence, we now know that this is not the case: the concept of neuroplasticity revolutionised our understanding. For me, just as a repetition of traumatic experiences has created a range of negative problems and habits, so repetition of positive inputs can rewire my brain towards a brighter future. I can actually influence how I think about and show up in the world – and that is nothing short of a miracle!

The more sobering news is that it isn't necessarily a straightforward or quick process. Changing deeply ingrained habits can require dogged perseverance, alongside a decent dose of compassion and patience with ourselves when we don't make progress as quickly as we had hoped we would.

I intend to put myself in the driver's seat this Christmas through some intentional practice – otherwise known as ritual.

Rituals tend to be associated with religions, and so can be less familiar to people who have never engaged with a religious tradition. I got married to Simon in our university chapel, where I had spent several years singing in the choir. It was a familiar, comforting and inspiring place for me, a place where I had participated in rituals, thought deeply personal thoughts, and prayed deeply personal prayers. So, it felt natural for me to take the biggest step of my life there. I can't imagine that it feels the same for people who get married in an unfamiliar building, whether a church or another location. It must feel more impersonal, and whatever rituals are performed in the ceremony must feel more alien.

In fact, in a non-religious context without ready-made rituals, some people can find it harder to journey through life. This can especially be the case when encountering key meaningful moments such as births, weddings and bereavements.

But rituals don't just have to be linked to religious belief. I first co-created my own ritual with a couple of close friends when I was sixteen. My parents had to travel away each weekend for work, but now that I was old enough and had a lot of studying to do, I had opted to stay at home in London. I remember walking out of the school front door on the first Friday afternoon of term, suddenly feeling lonely and wondering what I would do with the long evening stretching out ahead of me. I bumped into two friends who were also at a loose end. We went to a local café for chocolate cake, and I ordered a Diet Coke to wash it down. The café was a friendly place, allowing us to sit there for several hours chatting over one piece of cherished cake each.

This quickly became our Friday afternoon ritual. I remember how much I looked forward to it. I also remember how much we laughed, and how much my friends joked with me about how ridiculous it was to choose Diet Coke alongside a very calorific piece of chocolate cake! Although I didn't think about it in these terms at the time, this became a ritual that signalled the end of the school week and ushered in the relaxation and freedom of the weekend. It became a chance to wind down and bond together habitually.

We can all create rituals out of everyday things, in our own unique way. We can intentionally choose from a huge menu of options that exist in the world, and repeat what works for us. In the case of me and my friends, many of the other school kids back then wanted to go to pubs and clubs on a Friday evening – but it turned out that a café serving chocolate cake was just perfect for us.

We can get scared off by the notion that what we're doing isn't perfect. But, as with most things in life, it doesn't need to be. We can just get started and let the process unfold. Intentional practice will develop new habits, and we will learn as we go. This will rewire our brains in supportive ways and lead us to a new way of being.

So, we can make our own rituals. Rituals which serve us. And we can just get started in our here-and-now imperfect lives and see where the journey takes us!

For my part, I'm so keen to intentionally build a new personal doorway into Christmas, a doorway that leads me to a calmer, more joyful place! In contemplating how I want to construct my Christmas rituals and practices, I have discerned the potential of taking a holistic approach. I intend to use this process to liberate all constituent parts of me: my thinking mind, my emotional mind, my body and my spirit. I'm going to use tried and tested approaches as well as experimenting with new ideas and concepts, to challenge my preconceptions and find out more about what works for me.

So, let's dive in...

Part Three: The alchemy of my rituals

In which I discover how to liberate my mind, emotions, body and spirit this Christmas time.

Chapter 7: Getting started

Letting go of the outcome
It is a fundamental dichotomy that I have learned in life: to achieve the things we long for, we need to both make our best efforts to enable them to happen, whilst at a deep level also letting go of the outcome. It is an acceptance that we are not completely in control of our lives. Yes, we can absolutely orient ourselves in the right direction and take all sorts of positive steps to make our desires more likely to materialise, but their fulfilment is not within our gift. Ironically, I have found that, once I truly surrender the outcome, it becomes significantly more likely to happen – which can lead to crazy circular mind games if I'm not careful, but in essence the surrender needs to be real, heartfelt, meaningful. A deep exhale and release.

Which is what I did with my husband on 30ᵗʰ November 2022, to usher in the season of Advent which is the Christian period of waiting for the joy of Christmas when Jesus was born. I put together my own service to mark the occasion, including poems, readings and songs I had chosen for their particular significance to me.

We started off with a moment of quietness to calm ourselves from a very busy day, then we lit some candles to set the scene. We then honoured the little girl that I was in the past, the little girl that was wounded, receiving scars that I bear to this day. It was important that little Alexandra was present with us. We then acknowledged the hurt, and the fact that we were leaving the situation behind.

Then we focused on healing, with lyrics and readings talking about laying down one's internal baggage, and resting in the present. And finally we reflected on the joy we wanted to usher in for this Christmas season, focused on true love.

Now you could ask what the point of this was – after all, I could have just listened to songs and read inspiring quotes whilst I went about my daily business. But I found that there was something piquant and powerful in doing this more intentionally. Putting together the service helped me to think more carefully through the journey I wanted to reflect on, and gave me a reason to collate some resonant, meaningful words and songs as part of a broader tapestry. Obviously, there were no surprises for me as there would have been in a service arranged by someone else, but fascinatingly that didn't take away from the impact.

Actually, I felt nervous about the service just before we started. I felt silly and foolish, and almost didn't want to go ahead with it. But I decided to put those thoughts aside and take a chance on trusting the process. I wasn't disappointed. Standing together with my husband and giving our full attention to what we were doing added layers of meaning and contemplation. During one of the songs, I felt a desire to express myself more physically through dance, but felt quite inhibited – even though my husband was the only person in the room! Given all that I had learned about the importance of the body in healing from trauma, I tried to shake off my inhibitions and was at least partially successful!

At one point in the middle, there was space for my husband and I to reflect on how we were feeling and to express what we wanted to in this situation. I was surprised by the force of the different emotions I expressed, from white-hot anger, to the heartrending wave of sadness for difficult situations in the world, to warm thankfulness for the wonderful things in my life.

Having reflected on my journey and let my range of feelings out, I then let go of the outcome for the coming Christmas. While I deeply long for a joyful, laughter-filled Christmas and am weary to my bones of the seemingly never-ending journey of healing that I have had to take, I take the view that what will be will be this Christmas time. All I can do is show up with intention, orient myself towards the light, and aim to put into practice all that I have learned about healing.

It feels a bit like being a gardener who cares a great deal for the plants that they tend. There is so much that they can do to encourage a positive outcome, such as placing plants in the right kind of soil and in a conducive location, and giving them all the water and nutrients they need on a regular basis. They can tailor this as required: just like human beings, plants have similar basic needs, but with different nuances of what they require to thrive. Giving plants all this care makes it much more likely that they will grow and flourish, but this is never one hundred percent guaranteed – the unexpected can always come along and change the course of events in ways we hadn't anticipated, for good or for ill.

Healing feels even more like that to me, since I can't describe with scientific precision how the process unfolds. All I can say is that, looking back, I can see more clearly when and how my healing has progressed. And I have more trust now that the healing process that has started will complete itself – but I don't know exactly how and when that will happen. I'm more content with that uncertainty than I have ever been in the past.

Marking the start of the Christmas season in this way helped me to begin the journey of liberating myself to enjoy Christmas across the whole spectrum of how I experience the world. I liberated my thinking mind by reflecting on the journey behind and before me. I liberated my emotions by giving them a safe space in which to be expressed and honoured. I began to liberate my body through allowing myself some greater freedom of movement. And I liberated my spirit by reconnecting to the great goodness in the world that I believe in, by articulating my hopes and dreams, and by letting go of the outcome.

After we finished the service, we danced to some fun Christmas music that we hadn't listened to for a couple of years given my avoidance of the season the previous year. We truly let ourselves go, dancing as if no one was watching – which, luckily for both of us, no one was!!

I had started the journey, and I didn't know where it would lead me...

Be a laboratory

As I vowed to adapt existing techniques and try new things during this Advent period, it was important for me to think about how I would evaluate success, how I would decide what to carry on with and what to discard. We all know that we can try something once and think it has been a waste of time – but also that if we only give the practice a chance, it can grow on us. Sometimes the value of a practice only demonstrates itself over time, and we can miss out if we throw it away immediately in a knee-jerk reaction.

Meditation is a classic example of this phenomenon. So many people give up on this practice because they don't feel a discernible benefit within the first few sessions, and those first attempts to still oneself feel so difficult. But the power of meditation is in the repetition of the practice, learning to lean into it and discover a new way of being. Transformation is rarely immediate, we need to show some discipline to reap the rewards. Equally, we shouldn't be put off by assuming that only perfection will do. Simply showing up for a few minutes faithfully day after day is likely to achieve more than you could imagine at the start.

I decided that I would aim to experiment wisely. I would give new things a chance to bed in properly, and only take a quick decision to stop something if my intuition was strongly guiding me in that direction, like a warning system. I knew instinctively that this process would involve a careful balance of revisiting old traditions and introducing new ideas, but I couldn't tell you exactly how that would play out in practice.

Chapter 8: Liberating my thinking mind

Why do we talk so negatively to ourselves?
I used to believe that my thoughts were basically truth, coming directly from the core of me. I also used to believe that I had no power over those thoughts, that they were fully in control of me. It has often felt as if I'm on a flimsy life raft in the middle of a huge, tempestuous sea, seemingly totally at the mercy of my mind's waves of thought crashing down on me, as I hang on to safety precariously by my fingertips.

So, you can imagine that when I first came across the concept of positive affirmations, I was highly dubious. It had the distinct ring of self-help quick-positive-results-guaranteed mumbo jumbo. Surely just saying stuff to myself each morning that I wished to be true wouldn't just make it so? That was surely the realm of science fiction rather than science fact.

Well, it turns out that I've come on a bit of a journey with the whole affirmation concept. If you aren't familiar, an affirmation is simply a positive statement designed to challenge negative thoughts. We all have a stream of negative chatter going on inside our heads, which is linked to our evolution. In days gone by, our cave-dwelling ancestors did not enjoy the relative safety and security which we pretty much take for granted nowadays. They had to constantly watch out for life-threatening danger, particularly in the form of predators lurking in the shadows ready to pounce on them at the right moment. In simple terms, since those who survived to pass on their genes will generally have been those who were more alert to sensing and responding to danger, we are wired for survival. Wired to look out for threat everywhere. Ready to respond at the slightest whiff of potential danger. Fight or flight. Or indeed freeze and fawn, as I practised so expertly during my childhood.

Now, we humans don't face the same existential threats these days. Having said that, any woman walking down a dark, lonely street alone at night will know what it means to be constantly alert for potential danger. But a lot of the time we are surprisingly safe. However, our brain's wiring has not yet had sufficient evolutionary time to catch up with that revelation. So, we still look out for danger everywhere. After all, for our ancestors, just one false move, one lazy moment of not spotting the danger prowling nearby, could be enough to signal the end of their existence.

This caveman thinking means that we have a serious negativity bias. Focus on the negative, because the negative might kill you. Or more likely in the modern world, the negative might mean that you don't achieve your dreams, or manage to pay your bills, or land that longed-for promotion. We all know what this is like. "I'll never get that job – I don't have enough experience and I'm not confident enough." The trouble is, this negative chatter is now distinctly unhelpful to us in many of the modern-day situations that confront us. If you keep telling yourself that you aren't good enough for the job, chances are that you will arrive at the interview deflated and small, talking quietly, lacking confidence and stumbling over your words. Which then in all likelihood fuels a self-fulfilling prophecy. You don't manage to sell your experience well and you don't demonstrate confidence, so hey presto, you don't get offered the job, even though in reality you are extremely well suited for it.

I remember laughing when I read advice saying that, before an interview, instead of sitting quietly in the waiting room, you should go to the sanctuary of the bathroom and take on a heroic stance, perhaps planting your feet firmly apart, raising your hands defiantly into the air, clenching your fists and flexing your muscles to demonstrate your physical power. What a ridiculous notion! And yet when I tried it (yes I did!) I couldn't deny that it felt good, as long as I was absolutely sure no one was watching! A study bringing together the results of academic studies has shown that the main demonstrable benefit is found in having a neutral, open stance, rather than having a more expansive, powerful pose (Elkjær et al., 2022). Nonetheless, who doesn't want to act like Superman in the bathroom before an interview?! There's clearly more research to be done here...

This research is all about eliminating fear and generating confidence in the body, so that you enter the interview room exuding an air of assuredness. I have begun to think of affirmations as being similar fodder for the brain. Imagine if, instead of saying to yourself before that all-important interview, "I'll never get that job – I don't have enough experience and I'm not confident enough", you intentionally replaced that incessant negative chatter with positive statements that you could believe in. So not just something illogical like, "I am definitely the best candidate for the job", but perhaps "I have an impressive range of skills in my specialism", "I am confident in my abilities in managing a team" and "I have a track record in being assertive and presenting myself well in meetings".

If you repeat those statements regularly before the interview, your brain will drink them in so that they become front and centre of your thinking and your attitude. Which means that you will go into that interview with a mental focus on your assertiveness, confidence and breadth of skills. This will make it much more likely that you will present the best version of yourself, with positive body language and eloquent answers coming to the fore.

Does this necessarily mean that you will get the job? Well, no, of course not! In my years leading teams and mentoring people, I would always remind them that there are elements of the interview process that they can control – namely how they prepare for and show up at their interview – and other elements beyond their influence. They can't control what the recruiter is looking for, or who else has applied for the job. No matter how well you perform in an interview, if there is someone else in the pool who is quite simply objectively more qualified than you, they will probably get the job if they give a decent account of themselves at the interview. But if you go in there and give it your all, having prepared in all ways to the best of your ability, you will feel that you did everything you could possibly do and that will give you greater peace of mind, no matter what the eventual outcome.

No results are guaranteed in this life, but we can increase our odds of success by doing everything in our power to show up as the best version of ourselves. That is what I believe affirmations are all about.

But is there any proof that affirmations work?

In actual fact, there is! According to a 2014 review of scientific literature (Cohen & Sherman, 2014), well-timed affirmations can have demonstrable, lasting benefits for people in a range of areas including health, education and relationships. Affirmations work best as part of an overall system rather than in isolation, when they inspire us to take positive actions which are aligned with the outcomes we are looking to achieve. Nothing concrete ever happens in this world unless we actually take action.

But it is important that affirmations are not too positive and therefore unbelievable. I had reached this conclusion through my own experience, as I explain further below – but it turns out this is backed up by scientific evidence. If someone feels a particular deficit in an area of their life, stating overly positive affirmations relating to that area may actually serve to focus their mind even further on the deficiency they feel (Wood et al., 2009).

My Christmas affirmations

I'm going to share my Christmas affirmations with you, and the thinking behind them. Not because I think anyone else should necessarily use them, but because I think the process of crafting our affirmations is a personal one and I want to show you how it worked for me. There are lots of articles and books out there giving you ready-made affirmations, and that is fine up to a point – but I believe that a key ingredient that lends potency to the process is delving into some of your own negative and limiting beliefs and reframing them in a way that you can actually resonate and connect with.

For me, a lot of this is about overcoming my fears, particularly fears of irreparably ruining Christmas in my attempts to fix it this time around. The problem is, if I act from fear, I will simply avoid Christmas altogether – and that is no solution! So here goes...

Alexandra's Christmas Affirmation Number 1:
I let go and I follow God's light this Christmas time

This is an important affirmation for me which grounds all of the others that follow.

Just like going into an interview process, I can do everything in my power to orient myself towards the light this Christmas, but I can't completely control my experience of the festive season. I can increase my odds of a positive outcome by taking steps to play my part fully, but there are all sorts of external and unexpected events which could come along and influence the outcome. All I know for sure from past experience is that, when I hold on tightly to try to manage something within an inch of its life, it tends to become self-defeating. My own stress levels increase as I grip hard to control what is happening – and that in itself is quite often enough to tip the balance of my emotions, ironically resulting in me responding more negatively to things and having a lesser experience than I might otherwise have enjoyed. I have realised that my path to peace is to do my best in all things whilst also letting go of my dream of the outcome. After all, the unexpected may, much to my surprise, make things better rather than worse! If I can be open to whatever comes along, I am more likely to welcome it with open arms and extract the best possible experience from it.

This is also the affirmation where my faith comes into play. I believe that, even if I don't know exactly what's happening or how things will unfold, following God's light will eventually bring me home. Recently, some of the stories of Jesus healing women who had been sick for many years have spoken to me, for obvious reasons. "Take heart, daughter...your faith has healed you" (Bible (NIV), Matthew 9:22). Bring it on, I say!

Whatever you believe, whatever it is that guides you through this life, I think it is helpful to harness the loving power of that beacon in your affirmations.

Alexandra's Christmas Affirmation Number 2:
My brain is a mind-blowing creation which I can rewire through patient practice

I have found it truly heart-rending to come to the understanding that the events of my childhood literally wired my brain differently to what would normally have been the case. I'm more anxious, more on the lookout for danger, more prone to mental and physical illness. Before I understood this fact, I knew in my bones that something was amiss, but I couldn't explain why. I knew that I didn't approach life with the same zest that many others around me did. I believed that I was at the mercy of my mental state, that my outlook on life was fundamentally and permanently different.

Then over time I acknowledged the abuse that had happened to me in childhood, and I read about the imprint which that kind of behaviour leaves on a child. Everything finally made sense. But there was also great risk for me at that time: a risk that I simply gave up, believing that I was a victim of circumstance and that there was nothing I could do but accept my fate and suffer through the rest of my existence. This was often a very compelling narrative that nearly caused me to drown, metaphorically speaking...

But thankfully I was also learning the magical truth that we can rewire our brains through conscious, patient, diligent practice. Positive habit building is one method, stating affirmations is another. So, this affirmation in particular is reminding me that, whilst I could spend all of my time and energy this Christmas bemoaning what happened to me in the past, I also have the choice to harness the amazing features of the mind-blowing brain that has been given to each of us to point myself in a new, more hope-filled direction. Whilst it was undoubtedly important for me to acknowledge the wrongs that had been done to me, it was then equally vital for me to take steps to move forward from that place. I realised that I can literally programme myself to think and act differently to my current habitual patterns, and that is a veritable superpower! I wanted the truth of that superpower to properly soak into my subconscious through this affirmation.

Alexandra's Christmas Affirmation Number 3:
I am less anxious over time, and I step out despite fear so it doesn't control my destiny

This is an example of where I have been careful how I craft my affirmation so that I can actually believe in it. It is important for affirmations to be written in the present tense, otherwise they become vague aspirations that you don't really believe in or step into in the here and now. In this case, some people might choose an affirmation such as "I am calm and at peace, I have nothing to fear". But this sadly wouldn't resonate with my lived experience, so the statement would become empty words without proper meaning for me. From what I can tell at this stage in my life, I will always feel fear and resistance, and there absolutely are valid things to be fearful of in life. In fact, all of us face fear, it is a fundamental facet of the human condition. However, where we can make choices is in how we respond to that fear and resistance. We do not have to let them dominate us.

I can choose conscious practices to release tension and anxiety, thereby having confidence that I'm becoming less anxious over time. Whether I ever truly reach a Zen-like state is another matter, but to be honest I don't really need that to be the case! Whilst it would be quite the achievement, I would happily settle for a life with a manageable amount of anxiety, which is significantly less than the level I have endured up to now.

And I can step out each day this Christmas season, despite the fear that I feel, to reclaim the celebration that I love. It is powerful for me to decide that I don't want fear to control my destiny. I don't want to lie on my deathbed and think that fear dictated my decision-making and carved the path of my life's journey.

Alexandra's Christmas Affirmation Number 4:
I do my very best to react positively to everything that happens this Christmas time
Since I cannot control all that life throws my way, my power is in how I respond. My counsellor used to repeat this to me often during our sessions in years gone by. Truth be told, it was one of the few things

she said which really frustrated and angered me. Other people did bad stuff to me, and unfortunate things happened to me, so why should I be the one to respond positively? Why should I have to make that gargantuan effort? Why shouldn't it be someone else's job to fix the problem, perhaps God or even the person who caused the damage in the first place? I used to get all tied up in knots about why I shouldn't be asked to make this monumental effort, and how the world was frightfully unfair.

On one level, I still agree with myself on that point. But the uncomfortable fact remains that only I can choose where I go and what I do with the things that happen to me. Whether I like it or not, I have my hands on the tiller – and, because my brain is malleable as per Affirmation 2, I have a choice to make as to whether to navigate in a better direction. It was important for me again to state this affirmation in a way that I could believe in. Rather than "I react positively to everything", I cast it as "I do my very best to react positively to everything", which was the best I felt I could aim for at this time. Which is still a whole lot better than I have managed in the past.

Alexandra's Christmas Affirmation Number 5:
I focus on my many blessings, including the blessing of a fresh start in our new home
Sometimes it is really easy to overlook all the positive things in our lives. It takes effort to reorient our negatively skewed brains towards the blessings that are literally right in front of our noses. While it may sound cliched, it is nonetheless true that we are blessed to have clean water, abundant food, a reliable roof over our heads and walls and windows to keep out the wind and rain, and the kind of safety that our ancestors and many others around the world now could only dream of.

So, this affirmation encourages me to take time to notice my blessings, so that they properly sink into my conscious mind. And not just in a superficial way, but really clocking the details. Not only do I not need to worry about where my next meal is coming from, but my weekly menu is tasty, varied and nutritious. Not only do I have clean water to drink, but I can choose from many other flavoursome drinks besides.

And I have so much more to be grateful for. My faithful, generous and gorgeous husband. The handful of longstanding friends who really value, understand and cherish me, who make time for me when I really need it no matter what other pressures they are facing. The beauty of nature, from the Scottish hills I have fallen in love with to soaring trees, crystal blue lakes and silken soft meadows. The joy and freedom of vigorous exercise and feeling blood pumping energetically around my body. The comfort of my home and the treasured possessions I have gathered over the years, which trace the story of my life.

The more we focus on what is beautiful in the here and now, the more we notice and truly absorb the so-called "little things", the blessings that nourish us and collectively add up to a life well lived.

Alexandra's Christmas Affirmation Number 6:
I know that I matter and I have a loving, supportive community
For years after we got married, I would quiz my husband as to why he stuck with me during all the hard times, and why he loved me out of all the other human beings on the planet with whom he could have chosen to spend his life. And he kept gently replying, "Because you're you, and because you're wonderful!" Eventually, he would ask me to say the reply myself, to try to help it sink in.

It took me years and years to really believe that I mattered just because I existed. In my darker moments, I would often mull that the world would be a better, less complicated place without me in it, with my stresses that seemingly messed things up. But my faith would remind me that every human life is intrinsically valuable. I grew up believing that I was valuable because of what I achieved, and it has taken years to unpick that notion of earned value. Things finally came to a head when an injustice happened at work and I was deemed not to have performed to the required standard. Whilst I eventually overturned this judgement, since various important factors had been overlooked, it was the inward journey that I undertook during the dark period which was most transformational. For the first time, I truly appreciated that God loved me for who I was, not for what I supposedly achieved. It was a radical turning point in my life.

I'm so conscious that not everyone is lucky enough to meet their soulmate at a relatively young age as I did. But I do hold on to the belief that each of us has our guardian angels, in whatever form they may take. Those angels guide us along part or all of our journey. Beyond my husband, there are members of his family who have loved and supported me for many years, and friends from school and university who have stood the test of time. My long-term counsellor has provided faithful support and guidance. Whilst sometimes I wish that I had more soulmate friends living closer to me, I keep reminding myself how blessed I am.

I have put these two statements together ("I know that I matter" and "I have a loving, supportive community") because my true supporters will make sacrifices to support me. Christmas can often be a time of obligation – "We have to go and visit Aunty such-and-such", and "Grandma will be mortified if we don't follow tradition and come to the usual family gathering". We love our families and want to honour them at this time, but equally it can feel really wearing. This Christmas, it has taken courage for me to take decisions that serve me first and foremost, even if that might not have been exactly what other people may have chosen. Whilst this may sound selfish, I know how prone my buttons are to being pushed at Christmas time, so to give myself the best possible chance of healing, I need to make the environment as conducive as I can.

Fundamentally, this aspiration reminds me that I can and should take decisions to look after myself, whilst always of course being considerate of others. My close community love and support me in this journey of healing.

Alexandra's Christmas Affirmation Number 7:
The magic is built one step at a time! I know what to do today to reclaim Christmas

Sometimes it is really hard to see the whole path that will take us to our desired destination, and all we can do is intentionally put one foot in front of the other and have faith that we are headed in the right direction. Even then, it is really easy to get discouraged and decide that we can't see any meaningful progress and therefore we might as well stop trying.

This is not a clever move! Even small changes, repeated faithfully over time, can add up to staggeringly large ones.

With this affirmation, I remind myself that I can make great choices today that will keep me on the pathway to reclaiming Christmas. I also remind myself that I can trust my intuition to guide me – this is not all about logic, I also need to listen to my gut to understand what is important here and now to advance my healing process.

Alexandra's Christmas Affirmation Number 8:
God will finish what he has started in me. He will nurture me so
that I can nurture others

Just as my affirmations started with faith, they come around full circle. This affirmation is inspired by a Bible quotation which says that God "comforts us in all our troubles, so that we can comfort those in any trouble with the comfort we ourselves receive from God" (Bible (NIV), 2 Corinthians 1:4). This is a statement that I believe that what has started will be brought to completion. Just as a cut will generally heal properly in the right conditions, so I believe that emotional damage will also heal properly if we give ourselves a conducive environment.

This affirmation leads on from the last one: I can't see the whole path, but I am trusting that I'm going in the right direction and will reach my destination. I just can't know how long it will take me to get there, or the exact route I will take. That is all part of the exhilaration of life! The controlling past version of me has begun a transformation into someone who is more willing to embrace new possibilities and accept that I am not in complete control of this crazy life journey.

Equally, I believe that I am being healed so that I can support others in their healing journey. Again, I do not know exactly how this will take place, but the desire in my heart keeps me motivated and taking steps forward even when it is hard, even when the steps feel impossibly small. This journey is not just about making myself better, it is about picking up tools and experience along the way that I can use to help others get better too.

Reframing and visualising

A lot of what I have described above boils down to reframing the limits I have imposed on myself, overcoming learned helplessness so

I can see and capitalise on opportunities amidst the turmoil of life. It is possible to see the same situation through a completely different lens – for example, is the situation threatening, or does it provide opportunities you wouldn't previously have considered?

Another tool that is widely recommended is to visualise a positive outcome. The very act of viewing yourself in that scenario helps you to contribute to it actually happening in practice. You prime the mind for success. I will describe more in a later chapter how I used this technique during the Christmas period.

Learning how to help myself

We live in an age of unparalleled information. There are scientific studies galore covering so many aspects of wellbeing and healing. There are so many people out there whose mission in life is to help us to live better. There is a gold mine if we only have time and patience to seek it out and explore!

Equally, we live in an age of unparalleled misinformation. People who want to sell us stuff regardless of whether it is likely to benefit us. People who want to take advantage of our weaknesses and our problems. People who don't care what the truth is, they just want to gain an advantage over us or make a fast buck.

Add to that picture the inexorable fact that many of us are seriously time poor. There are so many demands clamouring for our attention. All of them seem pretty important. So how can we devote some of our precious time to figuring out what would help us to feel and act better in our lives? However vital the question appears, there is a veritable mountain of information and misinformation out there and we often don't know where to start.

That has described me for a very long time. I have been consumed by busy and important jobs, struggling to keep afloat because of the turmoil going on inside me. As a result, it has been almost impossible for me to devote enough time to navigate the information out there to find what might work for me. I have often been reliant on others to guide me with what they know.

Until now. At this point in my journey, I have become a voracious consumer of information. I'm so keen to find out from others – both from scientific evidence and from personal experience – what might help me to complete the journey that had previously appeared to be never ending. I have read many books on heavy topics such as trauma and anxiety, which have been very helpful to me. During this Christmas period, I have resolved to focus on more positive material – how to fully experience more of the good stuff that life has to offer, how to construct meaningful personal rituals, how to feel lighter.

It is so helpful to feed our minds with reliable information that can help us restore ourselves.

Chapter 9: Liberating my emotional mind

As someone who experiences a wide spectrum of emotions pretty strongly, how do I navigate this Christmas time, when my emotions are likely to be even more heightened than usual? Overall, I was determined to approach the season with acceptance of whatever came up. It isn't possible to feel gloriously happy all the time, but I think it just might be possible for me not to spiral deeper into depressive states, when I don't feel as joyful as I wish I did, or as contented as I think I should feel.

Actually, one of the features of this period that I hadn't been expecting was feeling rather numb quite frequently, which periodically turned into bursts of more extreme emotion. It has been pointed out to me that this bears a striking similarity to grief, not surprising given my recent estrangement from my father. Although, if I'm honest, I'm relieved and generally feel a lot healthier and happier since then, although one still grieves how things could have been, how things should have been... And when are those feelings more likely to bubble up than at Christmas time, when the importance of family is so emphasised and we all become a bit more introspective with our loved ones? So, I think my mind is probably using numbness to protect me from the full force of all the emotions that could erupt if left to their own devices.

In the past, I would have strong views about how I should feel at particular times and events. I now seem more able to accept what comes my way with a pinch more equanimity, so I have not railed against this numb baseline. Having said all of that, there has still been a range of more complex emotions to navigate during this period...

Working through something versus letting it go

I remember there was a particular fun song from a Disney film that I really loved. Mummy and I had watched the film together at Christmas time not long before she died, and it was one of those moments that brought particular joy and laughter. So, I shouldn't have been surprised that the song became problematic after Mummy died, because I so strongly associated it with her. I tried to listen to the album a couple of times, but when I got to that song, I disintegrated straightaway and immediately switched it off. It seemed impossible for me to move past this oppressive grief and sadness, and I remembered my father saying there were some pieces of music he could never listen to again after his mother died.

But something in me rebelled against this presumed outcome. I loved that song so much, and it reminded me of Mummy in such positive ways. Was there not a more positive, life-affirming way out of this dilemma?

So, I decided to try something purely out of gut instinct. I put that song on the stereo and I made myself listen to it all the way through. I was shaking, sobbing out huge tears, wailing through it. I remember asking myself why I was torturing myself in this way. I had to go through that awful process more than once... But then, out of nowhere it seemed, something miraculous happened. It was like the storm had finally blown itself out, and only beautiful serenity was left behind. I could now listen to the song with simple joy in my heart – joy that my mother had lived, that she had loved me so much, and that she and I had shared such fun times together.

I fought for that song, and I retrieved it. If you listen out carefully, you might hear me singing along to it as I bop in the kitchen while preparing a family meal!

That same conundrum faced me as I opened our boxes of Christmas decorations at the start of December. I hadn't seen this stuff for two years, and so much water had gone under my life's bridge since then...

For such a highly emotional person, I can be remarkably detached from stuff a lot of the time. I only feel attachment to certain objects that hold some kind of special meaning to me. But opening that box felt like more of a flood of emotion, because of the memories of Christmas past that were evoked. Over time, my husband and I have built up our own collection of Christmas decorations, and I have chosen themes and colours that particularly speak to me. These I welcomed with gladness, like meeting old friends again after a lengthy absence! There were some tears, but they were tears of happiness.

Then I got a shock as I delved further into one of the boxes. All intermingled with our lovely stuff were some bits and pieces from my parents. My childhood Christmas stocking, which had been my mother's stocking when she was a child. Full of years of family history, but way too much for me to handle just then – waves of sadness came over me and I didn't even want to pick it up. Then I saw some of the cute gift tags Mummy would buy – she loved funny, slightly goofy Christmas characters to adorn her presents to others! She wanted to spread the Christmas cheer, and I think this was the reason I recoiled from these as well. Since she never quite received the unadulterated joy of Christmas that she so longed for, these gift tags came with a heavy dose of melancholy. There were also some more recent decorations with a strong connection to my father which I had no desire to display as unpleasant reminders of a difficult situation.

I asked my husband to take the offending objects away and pack them in a different box so I wouldn't be surprised by them again in future. You might understand why I did that with the decorations that reminded me of my father, but you might ask why I didn't try to work through the emotions with the other objects which might hold more significance – the stocking and Mummy's gift tags, for example. I can't explain it to you completely rationally, but my gut feeling was that this would have been a step too far. For now, but not necessarily forever. Crucially, I didn't ask my husband to throw these items away – and believe me, there have been things that have been tossed into the trash in recent months to purge myself of certain unwanted connections. I can imagine being able to reconnect with those things in future, and perhaps even wanting to. But I decided to listen to my intuition and put them to one side for this year.

Interestingly, there were some other decorations which could have fallen into a similar category but didn't – some beautiful white reindeer that adorn our Christmas tree, which Mummy gave to me one Christmas Eve. Why are they not tainted with the same difficult memories? I honestly can't quite tell you, except perhaps that they weren't displayed at my parents' house since we would use them on our Christmas tree at home, so they became integrated with the more positive memories we built in that safer environment.

I let my intuition guide me in all of this – I'll revisit this more in a couple of chapters...

Dealing with powerful swings of emotion

I had been taught for so long that lots of my emotions were too strong – too strong to be comfortable for others to receive or respond to, too strong to be welcomed, too strong to be acceptable. But didn't that mean that I was defective in some way?

It came as a revelation to me that my high sensitivity was a recognised trait, a trait that bestowed advantages as well as the disadvantages of which others made me only too painfully aware. I instinctively knew going into this Christmas period that I would experience a broad range of emotions, wider still than my normal range because of the piquancy of the season which evokes strong reactions and memories, and because of the previous trauma which still lives in me. Our limbic system, or "emotional brain", can bring back the feelings associated with old traumas in a heartbeat, just like you're reliving the situation with all the associated rough emotions. This will often happen if a trigger brings the memory back to the surface, or if you're facing a stressful situation which bears some resemblance to that original event.

I knew that it was important to approach the Christmas season authentically, being willing to express my emotions in order to let them out in a healthy way, rather than bottling them up as I had learned to do in the past to preserve myself in the face of danger. But how to express darker emotions without causing the kind of damage my father had invariably inflicted in the run-up to Christmas? Whatever had caused his flip-outs, it was clear that emotions were at the core of the issue – perhaps it was the pressure to be happy at Christmas time which ironically led to the opposite happening, or perhaps it was some past Christmas memory casting a long and dark shadow in his mind, whether or not he was aware of it. I was clear that I didn't want to damage those around me as he had done in an effort to neutralise the negative emotions swirling around inside him.

But it is easier said than done when an emotional clamp tightens around your whole being. I had a chance to practise my desired behaviours sooner than I imagined in December. Having moved to a new location where I was hoping to set up a business, we had then begun to hear some disturbing noisy activity nearby, which made me worry that we had inadvertently chosen the wrong location. I have a terrible habit of catastrophising, and I immediately worried that all our plans were totally scuppered. I tried so hard to remain positive that evening, but eventually when trying to settle to sleep, all my fears and tears came out with a vengeance. I decided it was best to leave my faithful hubby to sleep (which, thank goodness, he did) and I came back downstairs to the living room.

I had previously planned to light a candle if I felt distressed, but this was too dark a moment for that. I was just not in the mood for candles. I opened my journal and did something I have never done before. I let rip. I ranted. It was a verbal tirade, written hurriedly and scrappily, sometimes with particularly meaningful phrases scrawled in big messy capital letters. I told God all the reasons why I was really frustrated and angry at him. I even diverged from words and just vomited a massive uncontrolled scribble on the page, noting afterwards: "This pretty much sums up how I feel about life." Amusingly, when I later checked my Bible app for that day's content, with a smidgeon of trepidation, the statement that jumped out at me was: "Talk to God about everything. There's nothing He can't handle. Go to Him." I copied this into my journal and commented: "Well, probably a good thing given what I just wrote...almost makes me wryly chuckle."

It was hard for me to seemingly desecrate my journal in that way. I almost didn't do it – similarly to the way we want our lives to look so perfect, on social media and in photographs. But I knew deep down that I needed to let this difficult stuff out. Without a filter. Without fear of who would read it. Without tempering the strength of my anger.

I found words to describe what I needed: "I need peace...I need the stress to STOP. I feel like I'm going to explode or just give up and either way it won't be pretty...Right now, I need Christmas to work and not be derailed by this...I need to feel purpose and drive, and I need to want to be alive, I need for my business to work and to feel more stable...I need to know it's going to be OK, to really feel it deep down and be comforted. I don't want to feel trapped anymore, particularly at Christmas..."

I even managed to name some things I felt thankful for, a step forward for me in an emotionally charged situation like this. I named leaving London for the Scottish countryside, my victories in a couple of particularly difficult work situations, and my amazing husband Simon, "who is quite simply the best human being I could possibly imagine sharing life with". It was a new experience for me to name things I was thankful for in a dark personal situation. But I had come to realise it was an important skill to learn.

Another important skill is choosing how one responds to a given situation – which is perhaps the only thing that cannot ultimately be controlled by someone else. I had read about prisoners of war who had managed to retain a positive outlook despite their horrible circumstances. Crikey, if they could manage it in their extreme situations, surely I could rouse myself to do something vaguely similar when faced with the comparatively trivial difficulties that were presented to me? Of course, one has to be careful with such comparisons, because they can lead to guilt which can too easily spiral into a feeling of inadequacy. That is not helpful, but it can be good to remind oneself of the heights to which human beings can ascend when faced with tremendous, seemingly insurmountable challenges.

I couldn't be happy in this experience, I couldn't even light a candle to contemplate the light. But I did manage something I hadn't done before – I found a non-destructive way to truly let my emotions be expressed, and then I genuinely started to feel better. I began to sense even in the midst of my gathering panic that perhaps I was overstating the risk. That has to be a meaningful step forward.

Afterwards, I felt able to settle down for a short period of meditative breathing. Amazingly, I was almost asleep before my phone timer went off. I gently crept up the stairs back to bed and fell asleep remarkably quickly. For a seasoned insomniac, this was nothing short of a miracle. Normally, when I'm unsettled, the sleeplessness lasts at least three hours. In this case, I was asleep within the hour. The next day, I was able to find greater equilibrium, particularly through exercising, as I discuss further in the chapter below about liberating the body.

I have also experienced several episodes where the situation with my father has caused me extreme anguish. Crying because I wish things could have been simpler, kinder, more loving. Longing for him to love me enough to remove the impediments to our relationship. Grieving for all the difficult stuff that has been, and for all the good stuff I have missed out on.

These feelings were triggered in various ways. On one occasion, Simon and I started to read A Christmas Carol, encouraged by various people who recommended it as being so Christmassy and evocative. Unfortunately, we were derailed by the first chapter. The depiction of Scrooge was, well... way too familiar. It was too evocative of something unhelpful: my father in his negative states, which we had both endured too many times. Whilst of course we were familiar with the story and knew that Scrooge is redeemed by the ghostly visitations that follow, that too would be hard to read, since it does not appear that there will be a similarly transformative event in my father's case. So, we took the decision to stop. Perhaps another year when things aren't so raw. Inevitably, even though we stopped fairly quickly, emotions had been stirred and I found myself crying over my dinner. I am learning that suppression is not a healthy or effective strategy. I need to let these feelings out properly before I can let them go.

Another time, I felt serious pent-up anger and tried to run it off on the treadmill. Unfortunately, I found that this didn't work – running is actually quite a controlled activity, as you need to regulate your breathing in order to keep powering your muscles effectively. I stopped and still felt seriously stressed, but I knew Simon was dealing with a problem and didn't want to aggravate him. I felt like I was muzzling myself, so I did the only thing I could think of to release my tension – I air punched as strongly as I possibly could! In retrospect, some kicking might have been helpful as well. Amazingly, this did the trick and my tension eased. Later on, when Simon's problem was fixed and we were sitting together in the dining room, I gave him some warning and then yelled a few times at the top of my lungs! Interestingly, the stress was over by then, and in the past I would have thought this wasn't necessary. But now I was conscious of my learnings around pent-up stress in the body and, I have to admit, it felt liberating!

What to do on down days?

In the run-up to Christmas, I experienced a couple of really down days. I didn't sleep well, I lacked energy, I felt blue. In that state, it is easy for me to spiral. Being surrounded by Christmas sparkles doesn't sit right on days like this. My inner critic tells me that I shouldn't feel like this, that I'm wasting the joy of this season, and it asks me why I can't just pull myself together and have fun like a normal human being.

But I know from bitter experience that the spiral isn't helpful. It turns a down day into a day with arguments, stress and bitterness that are hard to row back from. In fact, as I lived through these down days, the situation reminded me of my father in the run-up to Christmas. Whatever caused his darker mood, he allowed the Thundercloud to appear, rather than finding a healthier way to live through those moments without causing undue damage to himself or those around him.

I managed to hold a greater acceptance for how I was feeling. I have found the Buddhist teaching of impermanence particularly helpful in recent days. Nothing lasts forever, neither the good stuff nor the bad stuff – so don't grasp hold of the good, and don't try to push away the bad. Neither strategy works, and both lead to heartache.

So, I did what felt right on those two down days, and I didn't push myself to feel how I didn't feel. On the first day, I managed to rouse myself enough to go for a walk in the countryside with my husband. We didn't choose a strenuous walk, but a more manageable one which would soothe rather than exhaust me. It was the last of a string of snowy days, and I found a peaceful joy seeing the ice formations on the local lake. When we got back home, I spent the rest of the day reading. I wasn't as focused as I usually would be, and I could have found that intensely frustrating. Instead, I breathed deeply and accepted that sometimes things aren't exactly as you would wish them to be – but at least I was learning something, even if not at lightning speed. I was making the best of my circumstances, and moving forward.

I carried on this pattern into day two. The lethargy was still there, but I did a gentle run and spent the rest of the day clearing some admin that needed my attention. Not the world's most exciting activities, but they needed to be done sometime. I have a habit of storing up some non-urgent admin work for those days when I'm not motivated to do much else. At least then I use my energetic days for more powerful, creative work, and I have something available for me to fall back on when these lesser days arrive. It helps me to accept what is happening, because I'm still moving forward.

By not getting myself all stressed, I managed to settle to sleep at the end of day two of my blue period, and I woke up the next day much more able to engage in fun, stretching activities. If I had allowed myself to spiral into deeper darkness, it would have taken me longer to recover and get back to what I wanted to be doing. I think that in the past, spiralling wasn't always a choice, it was something that happened to me because of the circumstances I had lived through. But now I'm learning to harness my responses to better effect, and that is satisfying, even on a down day.

Absorbing the positive

What I have described before has all been about managing the more difficult aspects of my emotional range. But I was yearning for a more positive expression of my emotions as well. How could I learn to really dwell on the happy stuff, as well as working through the difficult stuff?

We all know what it's like to focus on the negative. Have you ever had an appraisal at work where your manager praised you for ten excellent things, but all you could think about afterwards was the one negative piece of feedback you received? It can take literally ages to shake those negative vibes off, and often the intervention of a loving friend or family member is required to help you regain a sense of perspective.

We focus on negative things as a result of our survival instincts, so it can take some practice to dwell more on the positive, to really savour the positive experiences that come our way, so that we properly enjoy and remember what good emotions feel like. And what about intentionally going on the hunt for new positive experiences?

When we do this successfully, it can create shining memories that we can draw upon in harder times. Frankly, the more of these we have, the better! For example, when I feel low about my abilities, I can draw upon the awesome experience of receiving a standing ovation for a concert I gave at university. As a child, I used to literally run off the stage after giving a performance, too embarrassed to face the audience. But by the time I was a young adult, I had learned to enjoy people's genuine expressions of appreciation, and I could just let all the positive vibes sink in and savour the moment.

This was a good example, but all too often I do a whole load of hard work to achieve a positive outcome and then don't really revel in that outcome when it materialises. So, I felt that it would be powerful for me to focus on the positive this Christmas.

One day in mid-December when I was feeling a little blue, I reset myself with a restorative, gentle walk and came back resolving to focus on the positive. I made myself a winter spiced hot chocolate to accompany me as I finished reading a book. Instead of just gulping it down without thinking about it as I often do, I savoured the milky, chocolatey taste of the drink, really giving myself time to feel the spicy warmth of it. I noticed the warmth of the cup as I cradled it in my two hands. I loved the fuzzy robin on the mug I had chosen. I revelled in my glasses steaming up as I lifted the mug to my lips. I then allowed myself to indulge in a few luxury chocolates that we only buy at this time of year. Again, rather than devouring them as my craving would so often lead me to do, I bit into them slowly, relishing the contrasts of the crunch and the smoothness, the caffeine hit and the strawberry tang, the sharp and mellow flavours.

Later that day, my husband and I had a little party together. He lit a fire in the open fireplace, we danced to groovy Christmas tunes, and we tried a new Christmas activity – reading a Christmas story aloud by candlelight. I loved watching the flames flicker as we read from JRR Tolkien's *Letters from Father Christmas* – delightful letters he wrote for his children from Santa, with particularly amusing anecdotes of his supposed helper Polar Bear causing various mishaps! I adored the hypnotising fire with red-hot glowing wood, and I had a hands-down fantastic evening with my best friend.

It is new for me to focus on joy, since I have spent so long managing pain and anxiety, expecting the worst to recur as it has done before. It doesn't surprise me that I still feel a fearful tinge, and yet I now feel a novel, quiet confidence that all will be well. On the one hand, my journey towards healing and wholeness feels fragile and potentially fairly easy to derail. On the other, I somehow just know that everything will sort itself out...

Chapter 10: Liberating my body

I mentioned earlier that I haven't been used to thinking much about my body, except as a means to an end. This experiment has been particularly insightful in helping me pay more attention to my body – this wondrous vehicle that allows me to journey richly through this multi-faceted world. I have learned to tend to it in some quite different ways, from sitting in silence to dancing wildly in my living room!

My lungs

I have always loved singing – from traditional choirs to glitzy musicals to Gilbert & Sullivan operettas. Anyone who is remotely serious about singing has to learn the correct way to breathe, since performing songs with aplomb necessitates not gasping for air at random points in the middle of a musical phrase. In a choir, you can all cover for each other in more challenging sections – I remember the wonderful sense of community in university choirs as we would actively listen out for each other and compensate our singing accordingly so that everyone could catch a breath without ruining the overall effect. Nonetheless, it's far preferable in general for singers to train themselves how to gather in enough air to last them rather a long time, as dictated by the music.

So, from a young age, the vital importance of breathing with the diaphragm was drilled into me. The diaphragm is a dome-shaped muscular partition separating your thorax (home to your heart and lungs) from your abdomen (home to your digestive system and other major organs). When the diaphragm muscle contracts, it increases the volume of the thorax which allows the lungs to fill with air. What you see visibly is that, as you breathe in using your diaphragm, your belly will move outwards to ensure that the organs in your abdomen don't get squished too much. However, many people do not make very good use of their diaphragm and take shallow breaths by expanding their chest. This means that they don't take in very much air each time and have to breathe much more often to compensate.

Despite my choral training, I am aware looking back that my breathing has been pretty unhealthy outside of choir practice as a result of the stress I was under at home. For many years, I was unaware of the reasons for my distress. Once I did become aware, I believed my problems to be mental and emotional ones. I knew that I felt physically unwell but did not necessarily link the phenomena. One of the ways that emotional challenges can manifest in the body is disordered breathing, which it turns out has lasting knock-on implications for our overall health and wellbeing.

A number of years ago, my counsellor introduced me to Christian meditation. At its core, it involved sitting up straight, closing your eyes, breathing in and out slowly, and contemplating a simple Christian phrase. I'm going to level with you – I was truly rubbish at it. I found it almost impossible to sit still without getting all fidgety, possibly because I wasn't properly at peace, and possibly also rebelling against myself in some way because I'd been so good at sitting still when required to do so during my childhood. I struggled to concentrate, my mind filling rapidly with all sorts of inane chatter and scattered, distracting thoughts. And then after a short while I used to be extremely frustrated to find myself dozing off! Much though I instinctively felt that the practice was a meaningful one for me, I couldn't develop a consistent routine. But it was something that I returned to fairly frequently over time and, even if I was nowhere near to becoming a great meditator, I at least began to teach myself how to take longer, slower breaths.

In the past few months and during the run-up to Christmas, I have returned to this meditative breathing practice more regularly as part of my morning routine. I have moderated my expectations, with five to ten minutes being a less daunting target than the twenty minutes I previously used to ask of myself. I've become less concerned about the thoughts swirling through my head, more able to view them as one of the inherent joys of being a human being. I find that this practice helps me to focus before taking on a meaningful task. It helps me to calm down if I'm worked up about something. It helps me to regain perspective.

But you might wonder how something as simple as breathing could possibly have such a profound effect. And it really does, even though most of us rarely think about this particular bodily function! Humanity clocked this a long time ago, which means that breathing features in many spiritual practices and traditions. This includes Buddhism: just before he died, the Buddha encouraged taking refuge in ourselves, rather than in external things.

In a nutshell, the reason breathing is so powerful if harnessed correctly is that, while it often happens unconsciously – good thing too, otherwise we might forget to take a breath and keel over! – we can also take conscious control of how we breathe. This is not the case with many other bodily functions. We can't instruct our heart how and when to beat and pump blood. We can't tell our digestive system how to process the large meal we just ate. And we can't govern how our kidneys filter out waste and toxins. The list goes on... But it turns out that we can influence how our body operates through our breathing. And by doing this, we can cultivate deeper awareness, become healthier, and even heal from past difficult events. While there are people who dedicate their lives to their breathing as a spiritual practice, we can all participate in this healing work in a way that feels meaningful and manageable to us.

So, how does our breathing influence our body more widely? It turns out that you have several basic states of being, the two most obvious being an active state in response to a perceived threat and a relaxed state where there are no threats in evidence. In the former state, you are amped up with energy, feeling a tension which enables you to fight or run away from the threat at a moment's notice. Because of the survival imperative, your body directs much of your available energy to these actions. In the latter state, without this need to be on alert, your body can focus on relaxing, digesting food, and repairing itself, activities which also require energy. We actually need to experience a healthy mix of these two states in order to function effectively. For example, whilst the relaxed state might sound like the more beneficial one, it can also be helpful to be in the more active stance to be motivated and primed to achieve great results towards a pressing work or life goal. But what is not helpful is to exist in one or other stance for much of the time. And one key hurdle we face is that our brain can't distinguish between real and perceived threats. So, if we are trapped in a bad situation from the past, or worrying incessantly about the future, our body spends a disproportionate amount of time responding to the stress that our thoughts create.

Our breathing varies depending what state we are in. The stress-filled active state is often more associated with shallow and rapid breathing, while the relaxed state involves – you've guessed it – slower and deeper breaths. If we've been more exposed to stressful conditions in the past, our natural breath may be shallower, faster, and less healthy as a result. But the good news is, because we can choose consciously how we breathe, we can retrain ourselves and this will have a meaningful impact on how we feel. Cool, huh?!

The first step is to become aware. As I have focused on my breathing this Christmas time, I have discovered that, whilst I was rather proud of my slow, deep breathing during morning meditation, things go rather awry when I'm not consciously directing how I breathe. When I'm just going about my day, my breaths are more restricted and shallow. Further than that, I caught myself on multiple occasions unconsciously holding my breath and pulling my belly muscles in tight for a chunk of time. It seemed to correlate with when I was concentrating really hard on something. We also naturally tend to hold our breath when we're afraid.

I have also begun to appreciate just how vital it is to breathe through my nose rather than through my mouth. I seem to have particular issues with this at night and when talking and exercising. Mouth breathing is bad for us in many more ways than we may at first appreciate. The air going into our lungs is not being properly filtered when it comes through our mouth. It isn't being properly warmed through the longer nasal passages. And crucially we don't release nitric oxide which has a myriad of breathing benefits.

These unconscious bad breathing habits of mine mean that my body is not functioning optimally. My breath has been marching me inexorably into a permanently more stressed-out state for years. Shining a light on how we breathe when we aren't paying attention gives us huge insight into our real state of mind and body.

I have started my journey towards better breathing. My singing and those faltering forays into meditation in years gone by have, I believe, saved me from truly crippling breathing habits that could have emerged from the trauma I was facing. But I am left with a legacy of a poor breathing technique which will not naturally improve unless I focus on it. My meditative breathing this Christmas time has helped me to feel calmer much more often than I would have done in the past. As I have relaxed my whole body on my long, slow out-breaths, I have often felt twitches in my body, particularly in my legs and around my eyes. People can find these sensations disconcerting, but the received wisdom is that they are signs that the body is being allowed to relax more deeply than usual and is starting to release long-held tension. It is the process of untying habitual stressful knots.

It can also be extremely helpful to spend ten to twenty minutes doing what is called a progressive muscle relaxation exercise. While sitting or lying comfortably, you breathe long and slow while focusing on contracting and relaxing muscles in particular parts of your body, one at a time. Breathe in and contract, breathe out and relax. Start perhaps with your feet and move gradually up to your shoulders and face. This simple exercise will help your whole body to release tension. I have used this exercise to great effect in the past, although it has felt like less of a priority for me at this stage in my healing journey. I have found it interesting to notice that we all have choices to make and never enough time – there are always trade-offs between different potential priorities.

Despite all of my breathing practice, I still tip rather too easily into a stressed-out state. So, I have more conscious breathing practice ahead of me to achieve optimal bodily performance, which will feed through even more positively into how I think and feel.

Moving intentionally

I have always been a fast, purposeful walker. On busy London streets in the past, you would have seen me jinking in and out of the crowds, determined to keep going at the pace I found comfortable and not settle for the group's slower, rather irritating amble! This type of walking was probably good for my fitness levels, but it did nothing for my state of mind and body. In fact, I would often feel quite stressed when surrounded by lots of people.

As a child, my parents would often have to gently cajole me to come out for a walk in the countryside. We walked along canals, country roads and beaches which were ostensibly rather lovely, but it wasn't an activity that grabbed me. Then I remember a family holiday to Canada when I was a teenager waiting for my GCSE results. My parents largely remembered that holiday for the incessant rain that fell on us. I remembered it for the awesome majesty of the Rocky

Mountains, which I found to be undimmed by the dampness. I was transfixed by their character, their grandeur, their different moods as the weather shifted. We didn't go for any big hikes, but the seed had been sown in my mind...

Roll forward about ten years and my husband took me on my first few mountain hikes on holiday in Scotland and France. I began to get the hillwalking bug. We trained ourselves rather more intentionally in the Welsh Brecon Beacons, and started to tackle some bigger hills on our regular Scottish holidays. And then came the inevitable moment when I began to aspire to become a Munroist. Scottish Munros are hills which rise 3,000 feet or higher above sea level. There are 282 of them. Aspiring Munroists aim to climb them all. Suffice to say that, despite the immensity of the challenge, especially given that we lived in London at the time, we had finished the lot within seven years!

There is just something magical about hillwalking for me. I could probably write a whole book on hillwalking metaphors that parallel our life's journey... Most people think I'm slightly mad to devote so much time to stomping around the boggy, rough wilderness. And they have a point – it is tough, demanding and energy-sapping. You can get very, very wet, tired and discouraged at times. And yet the joy of travelling through a natural landscape at human rather than car speed is something I wouldn't give up for the world. The rough terrain slows me down as I watch my step and pick my way. I also have to pace myself in order to conserve my energy for the multiple hours of walking ahead of me. The landscape changes around me, but slowly, giving me time to observe and absorb more detail of the wonder of nature. You will often see me crouch down in the springtime, taking a photo of the tiniest and loveliest of Scottish wildflowers that one would normally walk straight past, or even crush with one's walking boot without thinking.

Of course, my husband and I chat together on these walks – but we are pretty introverted and, even with our common interests and shared life, we generally can't maintain a constant conversation during an eight-hour hike. So often we will fall into a companionable silence, letting our thoughts gently mull in our minds as we concentrate on our footsteps and take in the surroundings. It is fairly common for us to solve a knotty problem on a walk, or come to a helpful new realisation.

So, I instinctively came to understand the meditative properties of walking. I felt deeply connected with my body and at one with the world around me. I was anchored in the present moment. And I had space and time for my thoughts to calmly marinate. But I would never have used the word meditative, because I'd been taught that meditation had to involve sitting still. So, you can imagine the 'aha moment' I had when reading about Buddhist meditation and discovering that this included the concept of meditative walking! All the pieces fell into place in my mind.

I have used this practice more intentionally this Christmas. One afternoon in particular, I was feeling very perturbed and distressed. All I wanted to do was settle myself, but I had failed to do so indoors. So, I donned my boots and decided to take a more focused meditative walk. This meant slowing down my usual pace. I consciously connected with my footsteps, feeling the comforting solidity of the earth beneath my feet. I slowed down my breathing. I noticed details of the landscape around me. I also recited my Christmas affirmations several times over, in time to my walking beat, focusing on those which resonated with my current feelings. That practice transformed my mindset for the day. As I came back home, I found myself able to relax with a calm spirit.

Another time, I walked up our local hill in the snow and felt tension in my belly about various stresses to do with Christmas. I worried that I was ruining the walking experience. You might recognise that crazy sense that we are sabotaging our own happiness in the moment simply with the thoughts running rampant through our heads. Here was the beautiful outdoors, made temporarily even more gorgeous by a dusting of snow, and I was ruining it by ruminating. In the past, I would often have spiralled downwards at this point and the day would have become irretrievable. But this time, I consciously noticed and named my feelings and worries, trying not to judge them. I brought my Christmas affirmations out of my mental toolbox again, and repeated them gently to myself. I focused on the positive things I had managed to achieve that day, despite various setbacks. By the time I got back home, I was in a much better state mentally, and was able to go out for a lovely dinner with my husband.

So, it seems that walking can have powerful restorative properties when approached with a meditative mindset. I have also found more recently that I can have a similar experience when running on my treadmill. I can run for much longer than I used to be able to, and I don't have to be listening to a podcast or watching a TV show to get me through it. Sometimes I can just enjoy the rhythm of putting one foot in front of another whilst gently focusing my gaze on aspects of my surroundings and allowing my thoughts to flow through me.

Free movement

I've realised that walking and running are fairly controlled physical activities. I have to manage my breathing and my pace carefully to ensure I don't burn myself out. There isn't really space to express oneself when running. This realisation led to me to think this Christmas that there might be a form of connecting with my body that I had disregarded in the past: dancing! True, I'd always enjoyed a good Scottish ceilidh, but I began to muse about the potential for more expressive dancing to help me demonstrate and release some of my more powerful pent-up emotions at this time.

I realised pretty quickly that I wasn't interested in learning formal dance moves – some YouTube videos made it abundantly clear that this would take extensive time and effort, and I wanted quicker results. What I felt a strong desire to do was to let go, to try out new things, to really dance like no one was watching! I found a dance therapy course online and decided to give it a go – definitely with no one watching me, not even my husband... In the initial limbering up exercises, I enjoyed the creativity of allowing my movement to take me where it wanted to. I enjoyed intentionally feeling different parts of my body – my palms pressed skyward, my arms feeling expansive space around me. I tried out a dance about self-acceptance. It had a South Asian feel, different to anything I had done before. I felt totally uncoordinated at first as I tried to follow the instructor's movements, but I built in confidence as I practised. Once I had the movements sorted, I could focus more on enjoying them. I felt empowered, expansive and uninhibited.

So why is dance so powerful? Well, alongside getting our blood pumping, it's a great way to express emotions by moving our bodies, including perhaps those more complex emotions that we are often encouraged to suppress. Dancing also brings the mind into the equation, as there are moves and routines to learn and master, and a real need for spatial awareness.

I found myself attracted to more improvised dancing, taking a song that I loved and just going with whatever I wanted to express at the time. This felt even more creative and freeing to me. It was less planned, and I could tap into the calm inner voice of my intuition.

I discovered great joy in improvised dancing this Christmas. I have danced to demonstrate feelings of hope for the season, hope that I can turn things around and feel different this time around. I have danced to heighten my feelings of happiness and excitement, giving them fuller expression through expansive movement. I have experienced a deeper connection with songs that I love, by dancing with them as well as singing along to them. I have communicated with my body what the song is emoting through its lyrics and melodies.

Sometimes I have just let it all go, trying some wacky moves just for the sake of it, just because I feel like it. I have lived my life in such a controlled way up to now that it can feel weird to let go and experiment. But I have given myself a safe environment where I don't have to worry about being judged by others, which has given me a new freedom.

And sometimes my husband has joined me on the living room dance floor. Dancing with others, particularly those you trust and love, adds a whole new dimension to the experience. Over this Christmas season, I have felt more and more able to just be me as I dance with him, and to be comfortable with him seeing that. And of course, we interact with each other as we dance. We feel each other's energy, we take cues from each other to synchronise or complement our movements, and we take inspiration from each other's ideas.

I have genuinely felt myself growing into a fuller, freer version of me by exploring dancing and movement this Christmas time. I have started to own the space around me with greater confidence. And I'm proclaiming more honestly with my body who I am, what I'm feeling, and what I hope and believe in.

Chapter 11: Liberating my spirit

I have said it before but it bears repeating – this section is not about me telling you what I think you should believe. Rather, it is just to show you how I have connected with my spirit during this Christmas period, in the hope of inspiring you with ideas of how to achieve something similar in your life. I believe that our spiritual dimension is a crucial component directing how we respond to the world, so it is good to be aware of what we believe and where those beliefs are taking us.

Focusing on the light

I have ignored candles pretty much my entire life. The only memory I really have relating to candles was during my honeymoon with Simon, when we were staying at a hotel in northern England. There was a power outage, and everyone was given candles to see where they were going and what they were doing. Instead of finding this helpful or even romantic, all I could think about was that the hotel was largely constructed of wood, and there was a high likelihood that we would all burn in our beds as someone carelessly dropped or otherwise misused their candle. So, not a high attachment to candles then!

Until now. It is safe to say I'm currently fairly obsessed by candles. I can stare at them for ages, almost hypnotically – I love how the dancing flame waxes and wanes, in a dynamic relationship with the air around it. Sometimes it seems to stretch up as if trying to touch the sky, sometimes it quivers and trembles in response to a passing breeze, and at other times it seems to hunker down, content just to still be burning, to still be in the game. I love big candles burned over days, and small tealights that only last for a few hours, with all sorts of scents that I can waft – carefully! – under my nose. I even treated myself to a candle advent calendar.

Fundamentally, I'm deeply drawn to focusing on the light right now, having spent way too long dragged down by the darkness in my life. A darkness that for many years I could only feel as an oppressive shadow smothering me more and more over time. A darkness that I wasn't able to begin to articulate or explain. A darkness that just seemed to grow bigger and more ominous. Now that I have taken steps toward understanding why things are the way they are in my lived experience, it seems that I'm more able to contemplate the light. The light that just might be beckoning me towards the end of the tunnel that I have walked and crawled through for so long.

Light is an important symbol for humanity in various traditions. Think advent candles in churches, the multi-branched menorah of Judaism, and Diwali, the Indian festival of lights, to name but a few. We enjoy bringing light into the darkness, cheering up long dark nights.

And candles of course represent a huge leap forward in human evolution. The ability to create and control fire was a gamechanger for our ancestors, providing a ready source of light and heat so they could be productive for longer, keep themselves toasty, heat up their food, and protect themselves from danger.

Then much more recently, the discovery of electricity was a further gamechanger which has totally and utterly transformed our everyday lives. I love my creature comforts, for sure. And it is amazing to be able to turn the lights up bright at any time of the day or night, so I can see clearly and perform complex tasks to my desired timetables and whims.

But my soul is innately drawn to dimmer, more nuanced light. Light that doesn't dazzle so much as it gently brightens and warms. Way before my current candle phase, I have always adored sunrises and sunsets. I love the beautiful pastel colours splashed across the sky and reflected on the land, trees and water. I love the way they grow to a crescendo as the sun gets closer and closer to the horizon, whether approaching from above or from below. And I love that, much like the fabled snowflakes, no two sunrises or sunsets look identical. But most of all, I love the gentleness of it all – at the right moment in proceedings, I can look directly at the Sun without harming my eyes. I can look straight at that enormous shining powerhouse of energy that has enabled us to evolve into being and walk on this Earth, because its true brightness is being somewhat deflected away from my tender eyes. Those incredible eyes that could only evolve alongside the rest of my finely tuned, complex body because of the energy constantly streaming generously from our awesome Sun.

People tend to talk about and share pictures of the most stunning sunrises and sunsets they have ever seen – the ones that are truly electric, with bold streaks of orange and pink daubed across the sky by an exuberant heavenly artist armed with an enormous paintbrush, and a Sun that looks as if it is made of molten gold. Of course, I love those kinds of sunrises and sunsets, they are truly spectacular and inspiring! But I also love the quieter kinds. My husband and I went summit camping in Scotland earlier this year. I crept out of the tent at silly o'clock in the morning, and simply spent an hour or so wandering in contemplative fashion as the light grew all around me. It wasn't stunning, postcard-worthy stuff. Cloud was blanketing much of the valleys and lower slopes, with just a few hilltops peeking out above it. There were no glorious bands of colour decorating the sky. It was more of a calm, soothing, warming glow – and I drank it in as I slowly walked around the plateau where we had made our temporary home. It was probably the closest I have got to something resembling a meditative state.

By wonderful coincidence, I'm writing this chapter during a blackout, this time a planned one so that trees encroaching upon power lines can be safely taken down. I found myself frustrated when we learned about the work at short notice, focusing on the practicalities of a winter's day without light and power. Would my phone and laptop batteries last? Would I be warm enough? I filled flasks and hot water bottles in preparation. But I'm glad that I managed to move beyond those twenty-first century annoyances and preoccupations. My advent candle is providing me with practical light on a dingy, cloudy day. It is also giving me comfort that the light shines on unafraid, even when surrounded by darkness. Yes, of course it could get blown out, but that doesn't stop it from shining as hard as it can for as long as it can, until its energy source is fully used up.

Fascinatingly, power was just restored here and I have chosen to keep the lights off for the time being, content to remain in the tranquillity of the candlelit dining room. I have been drawn in by the vibe.

Of course, at some point I will move back seamlessly into the modern world with all its conveniences, including bright light at the flick of a switch. But this quiet moment has reminded me what life must have been like before all of that, when light was a precious resource and, beyond the long, dark nights, even the short winter days were rather dim. That really would have given potent meaning to the patient wait for the brightness and festivities of Christmas, celebrating the arrival of the light. This moment has given potent meaning to my patient wait for transformational healing, for that time when I know for sure that the rivers of tears are behind me, for the time when I can start to help guide others through their own darkness. Somehow, I know in the depths of my being that this time will come, and yet I can be simultaneously gut-wrenchingly afraid that it won't, that I will be trapped in this dark nether region forever.

I know that I need to keep tending to my internal light so that it shows up a little bolder, a light that I can count on to keep illuminating my path. Perhaps as I do that, I will become a little less afraid of the darkness. Perhaps the darkness that once felt so malignant will become less terrifying, less all-consuming, more benign. As the old Chinese proverb declares: "It's better to light a candle than curse the darkness."

All I can really do is tend and cherish my flame so that my light continues to shine in the darkness, until the new dawn arrives.

Navigating spiritual darkness

One of the distinct challenges of life is dealing with forms of spiritual darkness. This could be an area of life where we are not sure what's right or wrong. Or a time when we don't know where we are going in life. Or a time when we do know where we want to be going, but we have no idea how we are going to get to that place.

Have you ever tried finding your way around when there are no lights on and it is pitch black outside? It is completely disorienting. Humans normally rely so much on sight as the key sense to interpret what is going on. In the dark, you have to call on other senses and abilities much more – feeling your way around walls and objects, moving with heightened spatial awareness to avoid tripping over something. Whenever I do this, I am truly in awe of those who operate in this world with no or limited sight all the time – or indeed any of the senses that many of us take for granted.

But here is the thing. Having to operate in literal darkness forces us to practise using other abilities that normally aren't so necessary. It is just the same with spiritual darkness. We can't necessarily lean on the logic and problem solving which serves us so well at other times. If we truly want to grow as human beings, I believe we need to learn to walk through times of spiritual darkness without simply running back to the light again as quickly as possible. That knee-jerk reaction will not lead to growth.

I have faced two main types of spiritual darkness during this Christmas season. The first relates to journeying through a period of huge, tumultuous transformation and not being at all sure where or how it is going to culminate. I have dreams and a vision, but I have no idea whether or how I can achieve them. There are just too many unknowns. In the past, I have always needed a solid plan to get from A to B, from my current state to my new desired state. But this has meant that I have limited what destination B can look like. I have limited my potential destinations to those I know pretty much exactly how to achieve. Unfortunately, I have discovered that this is a fairly narrow strategy in terms of life choices, and none of the destinations I have reached so far in life have actually been states I have wanted to linger in for very long.

It has become clear to me that I need to dream bigger and aim further. I need to reimagine and reclaim Christmas, and I also need to reimagine and reclaim my life. But that means that my usual skills of logic and planning will only get me so far. Yes, they are absolutely necessary for this journey, but they are not sufficient. I have needed to learn to feel my way as if in a pitch-black room, because everything is new and alien. I have also needed to break the journey down into manageable chunks, because if I tried to think about the whole thing, it would boggle my mind and I would probably give up on the assumption that it is too hard and I will never make it. And that is exactly what you do in the dark as well. You have an aim: "I need to get to the other side of the room where the light switch is." But you have to pay far more attention to what is directly in front of you to become familiar with your immediate environment and avoid falling flat on your face.

The other type of spiritual darkness I have experienced this Christmas time is doubt relating to my father and whether I have done the right thing in estranging from him. Most of my friends and family members have been unfailingly supportive, as well as all of the professionals whom I have consulted, but I can easily start to judge myself and worry that I have wrongly and selfishly put myself ahead of him. I have discovered that this is a particularly potent worry at Christmas time, when all the prevailing narrative is around the importance of family and spending precious time together in this special season.

I have struggled in particular when I have imagined my father sitting at home by himself at Christmas. Because that is probably the reality. He has neighbours and a few friends, but he doesn't generally want to build strong relationships and wouldn't dream of spending time with any of them at Christmas. Am I a terrible daughter?

Prayer and meditation are key tools for me at times of spiritual darkness. And of course, prayer is generally associated with religion, so it is not something that everyone would naturally use. It is normally understood as asking God for what you want and believing that he will give it to you, but great prayer is a much richer practice than that. It also encourages us to see ourselves within a much larger and yet connected ecosystem, to explore how we really think and feel about things, and to be thankful for the wonderful stuff in our lives. Prayer is also about more than just ourselves. The act of holding other people in our prayers is a powerful way to build our sense of compassion and community.

Using prayer in this way as I mull over the darkness in which I find myself helps me to make sense of what is happening. It helps me to recall how I have made my way in the darkness before. It helps me to connect with the great spiritual force that I believe in, and to connect with others by praying for their wellbeing. This is not the realm of logic, it is the realm of the heart, the soul and the gut. Spending time in quiet reflection helps me to remember my place in this great universe – I'm valuable but small! And it helps me to apply perspective and wisdom to the issues that are bothering me. I can't quite explain how this happens, but it just does.

I have come to see that I need to trust that a higher power is on my side when it comes to achieving my big dream. I can't map out the whole pathway, but I can use all my skills to take the next step and the next step and the next step, with faith that my small steps will add up to a journey well made, and the destination reached.

And when it comes to my father, here is the realisation I came to as I mulled over the unsatisfactory nature of the situation. I'm undeniably happier and freer since our estrangement. I have been able to loosen bonds that were so tightly knotted in the past. I'm truly healing in a way that I simply don't believe would have been possible were he still in my life. Because when we were still in a father-daughter relationship, I would take a few tentative healing steps forward, but he would inevitably drag me back a step or two or three the next time he interacted badly with me. Looking back, I can see this pattern so much more clearly. It was the reason why I felt so hopeless, because I could never seem to make sustained progress towards a better life.

I also realised that, much though I fervently wished and prayed for a happy ending for me and for us, I couldn't control what my father believed a happy ending to be, and I couldn't control whether or not he chose a happy ending. I love those films with a redemptive ending – where good prevails despite all the odds, where evil is vanquished and the protagonists live happily ever after. But I had to choose to take the redemptive path. And, in the end, I had to accept that I couldn't share that redemption with my father, because he simply didn't want it badly enough. At the point when we estranged, there was a choice for him – he could have chosen to listen to what I was saying and decide to investigate further, to see if redemption was possible. But instead, he responded angrily, just as I have witnessed him react to similar situations in the past.

He chose his path, which meant that I had to choose mine. I'm finding redemption but unfortunately it is without him. If he were to have a real change of heart, I would absolutely be open to that. But right now, I need to remember that each human being holds the key to deciding how they will respond to the circumstances in their life, the challenges they face. No one else has the power to decide that for them. Someone can try to point them towards the light, but they cannot force them to walk in that direction.

This realisation is tough, but it has brought me peace and renewed passion for moving forwards towards my new dreams. I'm not being callous, I'm simply recognising my father's autonomy in life. He must choose his path and I must choose mine. In most cases, this can be achieved whilst maintaining relationship, even if each party doesn't completely understand the other. But in some cases, the chosen paths are so divergent that trying to hold them together becomes untenable.

Following one's intuition

Intuition is a concept that is hard to grapple with. It isn't like logic where there is a rational explanation for the solution to a problem; it is about listening carefully to what your soul is telling you. I think quite often we can drown out our intuition with our fears, with the clamour of everyday life, with the pressure coming from other people in the form of well-meaning advice. Don't get me wrong, sometimes that friend giving difficult advice is absolutely right – and if you are tuned into your soul, it will probably be quietly telling you so. But often the person who knows best how to solve your problems is you.

Again, don't mistake me, I'm not saying that we should discard professional advice. Where there is a tried and tested solution to a medical problem, for example, I absolutely believe we should take advantage of that solution. But in these areas where the solution is not so clear-cut, I believe we each have wisdom to know deep down what we truly need.

The trouble is, our small, inner voice of wisdom will not shout for our attention. True, it may gnaw away at us so we know something isn't quite right, but it often gets crowded out by the incessant chatter in our minds. You know, that annoying inner critic that just keeps talking, no matter what you try and do. Day in, day out. Night in, night out. That voice that tells you that you are stupid, that you will never manage to achieve your dreams, that everyone thinks you look ugly or act stupid. That voice that wears you down, telling you that you are not worthy, not good enough. It has all kinds of damaging and hurtful messages up its sleeve, and it knows exactly when to deploy them for maximum effect.

So, what is intuition? I would define it as the ability to know something without being able to give a comprehensive explanation. It's getting straight to the answer without all the usual logical steps. While the ability to reason is amazing, intuition is perhaps even more awe inspiring – particularly when it gets us out of a sticky situation where logic might not have been able to save us.

Trying to navigate our path away from former hurts and towards healing can be one of those sticky situations. There can be all sorts of well-meaning advice, so many remedies out there that claim to solve the seemingly intractable problem you are facing. But only you can know, through your intuition, what is likely to work well for you. Listening to that small, inner voice will help you tap into your wisdom. And sometimes, it will take you in a direction you simply weren't expecting!

We need to find ways to quieten our chatter enough that we can hear that inner voice. For me, this has been through a faltering practice of mindful meditation. I cannot claim that I am masterful at it, but I have done my best to persevere over the years. The main advice I would offer is not to give up because you think you will never become a Zen Master. So what? Perhaps that is just not in your destiny! But even spending a few minutes a day practising being still and quietening your inner chatter as much as you can will reap benefits that you cannot imagine.

In my experience, intuition tends to come upon me as a moment of searing clarity where I 'just know'. I just know what to do, what to say, what to think in a given moment. Sometimes it may not even make objective sense, but I just know.

One example that comes to mind is when I was suffering with the sudden onset of a mental health problem soon after my husband and I arrived in London to begin our careers. I was beside myself, worrying that I was going mad. I hadn't felt confident about going to my GP for advice. At that time, my husband and I were looking for a new church – with some trepidation I might add, since we had recently had a less positive experience which made us more cautious about committing to a new community. One day when visiting a particular church which would become our new spiritual home, we were having cups of coffee as is traditional after the service, milling about speaking to people we didn't really know yet. I looked at the female minister and said to

Simon, "That's it. She's the one who can help me. I need to go and speak to her."

I literally knew hardly anything about her. But my intuition turned out to be spot on that day. It transpired that Ruth was a trained counsellor as well as a minister, and since that day she has patiently guided me through a range of issues during the past fifteen years. Without her quiet wisdom and faithful persistence, I'm pretty sure I wouldn't be where I am now, taking great strides in healing the hurts of my childhood. And all because I listened to that still, small voice of intuition.

Now of course one needs to be careful with this. You could say to me, and I could hardly argue, that people could listen to and act upon what they believe is their intuition telling them to do hurtful, mean things, that evil dictators have an inner voice telling them to inflict terrible pain in the name of power and domination.

All I can say in response is that I believe love is the ultimate guiding force in this universe. It is stronger than anything else, and true intuition will only ever speak from love. The key test must be as follows: if you think your intuition is telling you to do something that will be detrimental to someone else for no good reason, then it is not your intuition. Sometimes true love needs to be tough love, but it is still love.

Naturally, I can't prove any of this. The young Alexandra who used to cling to the primacy of mathematics with its correct answer to any problem has had to appreciate through growing up that this world is more complex. If she had stuck with pure logic alone, she would not have made the progress that she has made. There are mysteries in this universe which we cannot fully understand, but we can learn to embrace love as the primal life force, and follow where it leads us.

Chapter 12: Was all of this necessary?

Did I have to do all of these new things in order to redeem Christmas? And how much difference has each of them made? Honestly, I couldn't tell you for sure. I had decided that my need for healing was so urgent that I had to try everything at once, and couldn't run a rigorous experiment to test each practice separately. It could well be that one of my practices was the key driver towards healing, and that others had no discernible effect. There is no way for me to know for sure. And as a scientist, I know that correlation is not causation. When two things change at the same time, it doesn't necessarily mean that one is 'cause' and the other is 'effect'. It could be correlation, meaning that they're both changing due to some other root cause – or it could simply be coincidence! And it's even more complicated to unpick with so many different practices acting as inputs to the experiment.

But there are scientific studies which seek to determine whether there is cause and effect acting through the sorts of practices I adopted. Thanks to these studies, we know that various practices do generally lead to improved outcomes. Meditation improves mood. Progressive muscle relaxation reduces stress. Singing in a choir lifts our wellbeing.

There are some practices that work nearly universally, and others where the effects are more conditional on the person undertaking those practices. As I have delved into a range of practices and self-help books in pursuit of my healing, I have become acutely aware of how much people seek to sell a single method as the key to progress. And I can understand why on one level – generally speaking, it is a method that has worked for them, so they feel able to endorse and explain it, and are keen to spread the message to others who could benefit.

That is all well and good, but we are self-evidently not all the same, and I believe that what works for one person may not work for all. Long bouts of meditation have never worked for me, for example, because I quite simply fall asleep – even if I sit myself on a relatively uncomfortable chair! That may well be linked to the chronic insomnia that leaves me exhausted at all the wrong times, but I have decided it is not something for me to fight, at least for the moment. I can meditate for five to ten minutes, and that has been enough over time to give me greater peace and clarity. This limitation may change in future – and every now and again, I try meditating for longer, just to see what happens. So far, no change...

So, I'm not suggesting that you try exactly the same practices as me – you are, after all, your own unique human being! I would, however, encourage you to approach your healing with intention, to expand your boundaries to be open to new ideas, and to quieten your mind so you can hear that wise voice of intuition inside you. These qualities will, I believe, help you to find your way on your personal journey of healing and restoration.

I do think it is important for us to expand our horizons across the different dimensions of healing: thinking mind, emotional mind, body and spirit. My intuition led me to this way of seeing healing, so I sought to find practices to minister to those different aspects of myself. It has felt integrated and powerful to bring these facets of me together. Just like a handyman would not try to do every job with a hammer, similarly I have been expanding my toolbox so that I can draw on the most appropriate tool for the issue at hand. Some tools are brought out on a very regular basis, others are more niche but still have a purpose, and others we discover just aren't useful for us. Like that potato peeler that I can't use because it hasn't been designed with left handers in mind. It is helpful for us to try out our healing tools and figure out which ones are useful to carry around with us on our journey. Once we have a suitable toolbox, we will become more adept at knowing which one to pull out when challenging situations confront us.

Often, I have discovered that the different dimensions of healing come together. Dancing to good music enabled me to express my emotions expansively through my body, and to connect with my spiritual side in a new way. Just repeating my Christmas affirmations in the morning was helpful – but saying them whilst walking mindfully, or whilst stretching after exercise, was even more powerful for me. I was toning my body and my mind at the same time! Simply practising my breathing every day was helpful – but breathing in a rhythm to a simple prayer phrase was even more powerful for me. I was toning my body and my spirit at the same time!

I often found that bringing together the different dimensions of healing involved creative thinking. Sometimes we can put in all the effort in the world, but we try too hard and it backfires. We absolutely need discipline and commitment, but equally we need to develop a sense of freedom to allow new experiences to come to pass around and within us.

One concept that it was very important for me to grasp is that healing is not a linear process, however much I might wish it to be so. Every day is quite simply not better than the day before. Sometimes we experience a slump. What really matters at those times is that we don't give up, assuming that all is lost. We can actually grow through that slump, and emerge bigger and stronger at the other side.

Imagine a surfer. As they start out with their new hobby, they try some easier waves successfully, other harder ones less so. Over time, they will gain in skill and experience, and be able to tackle generally tougher waves. But sometimes those waves will still engulf them because of the nature of the situation: perhaps slight variations from what they have previously experienced, or simply that they perform less well in that moment than they usually do. Perhaps a negative experience might hold them back for a while, knocking their confidence – but they work through it and come out the other side stronger and more capable.

I want to be like that surfer – but instead of water waves, I'm surfing the waves of my mind, emotions, body and spirit. And I do believe I'm beginning to master some more complex moves!

Part Four: So how did my experiment turn out?

In which I discover whether the rituals and experimentation have been worth it.

Chapter 13: Christmas

I would summarise my Christmas journey this year as healing, refreshing, and sometimes challenging – definitely not perfect, but also definitely a reclaiming of Christmas that I can build on in future years. I brought together the various elements of what I had practised during Advent to help me through the Christmas celebration itself.

It felt like Christmas proper started when we stopped work. We made a ritual out of it, dancing together to a couple of our favourite Christmas tunes and then eating a special cake. The next day, we hosted our new neighbours for a festive gathering. We had a lot of tidying and food preparation to do. Normally I would have dived straight in, and probably got remarkably flustered about something along the way. Realising the stakes were higher, I put my various learnings into practice and spent some time on me first. I did a run which always gives me a flood of satisfied feelings afterwards. I then did some exercises and stretches, saying my Christmas affirmations a few times as I did so. I also practised positive visualisation – I pictured both the preparation and the party itself going smoothly, with me really enjoying the experience. Actually, "seeing" things in my mind has always been harder for me than other forms of imagination, which almost put me off the visualisation technique, but I have realised that I can still get enough of a sense of what I'm aiming for, and that seems to be sufficient for the practice to work for me.

The party went brilliantly! I felt such a warm glow of satisfaction when it was all over. So, it was then a bit of a surprise when I didn't sleep well afterwards and then experienced a couple of rather blue days. In the past, I might have put pressure on myself to feel happy at Christmas time, and equally I might have allowed the sadness to overwhelm me because I didn't know how to contain it. It turns out the simplest way to contain such feelings is simply to accept them for what they are and acknowledge to yourself that they will pass, just as all emotions do. I reminded myself that there was no requirement as to how I should feel in the run-up to Christmas, and also that it wasn't surprising that I should feel a bit blue given that this was the period when I would have had to contend with the Thundercloud as a child – and indeed up until just a few years ago. I unburdened myself of any expectation, let myself feel what I was feeling, and chose activities that suited my mood. I did some learning by reading a couple of books. This quiet activity worked for me, which enabled me to work up to more fun activities, including with Simon – taking a snowy walk, reading Christmas books together by candlelight. Accommodating and reacting to my lower mood in this way – accepting it without allowing it to spiral downwards – meant that this period of time didn't feel hopeless or damaging, and I came out of it more quickly.

I then found myself focusing more on celebration. I danced! I started off with a couple of more contemplative, gently upbeat Christmas songs. Then the hubby and I dressed up in the evening for a more jolly Christmas dance – there's nothing like a twirly skirt to make me feel joyous and special! And so, I kept dancing while cooking our dinner. By the end of the evening, I found myself contentedly gazing at the various tealights I had lit, letting the peace and happiness of it all sink in.

Things just got better from there, even despite one of the perennial seasonal bugs giving us the benefit of their presence! We had a glorious sunny walk with soup and Christmas cupcakes overlooking a wonderful view. The next day we treated ourselves to a scrumptious Christmas afternoon tea at home, with more of the aforementioned Christmas cupcakes, crumpets shaped like Christmas trees (yes, they do exist!), scones and an assortment of jams. We made a thing of it, and the occasion made us feel special and jolly!

Suddenly, we found ourselves at Christmas Eve. In some ways, it felt like Advent had stretched out forever, and in other ways like it had passed in a flash. Time does play odd tricks on us... I was feeling rather emotional and unsure about what to do and how. What if I made a mistake and became ridiculously sad? I was painfully aware that it was ten years since the terrible Christmas Eve argument that I described at the start of this book. Ten whole years had passed, and my father and I had not succeeded in holding things together.

I held the question of how to spend the day as I went about my morning tasks, particularly wrangling with myself about whether I should listen to the *Festival of Nine Lessons and Carols* from King's College at 3pm on Radio 4. It was a tradition of Mummy's for as long as I can remember, and one that I love too, but on the other hand, perhaps I would just find it too much of a reminder of difficult things... Eventually, I decided to give it a shot, because I cared about trying to reclaim it.

Just before the carols began, I asked Simon to sit with me. We did five minutes of breathing and meditation, and then spent some time praying for other people. For my father, probably on his own this Christmas time. For other people with whom we had experienced troubles or difficulty. For friends facing particular challenges during this season. This was my way of bringing them to mind and then letting them go, so that I didn't continue to ruminate on situations that I can't control. I cried, but again it was relatively contained, and this preparation actually left me feeling refreshed rather than bogged down.

As the carols started with the spine-tingling *Once in Royal David's City* solo, I lit tealights in the living room. Simon and I wrapped our presents while the service played. Some of it was so familiar – the readings telling the Christmas story, the carols that I know by heart. I did cry at times – the choir sang both of my mother's favourite pieces

– but they weren't hopeless tears. I think Mummy would be so delighted that I'm finding a way to love Christmas again, as she did.

After dinner, I had fun carrying a candle up the dark staircase and singing the *Once in Royal David's City* solo myself. This is a solo I have sung a number of times in the past in Christmas services, but I chose not to be part of a choir this year as I wasn't sure how I would feel. Singing by candlelight was magical! I then read Simon a short Christmas story I had read the day before. It was Jeanette Winterson's *SnowMama*. I didn't expect to cry but I did towards the end, because of the poignancy and kindness of it. I let myself feel the pain of my father choosing not to come back to me. But I have found my redemption in my husband, wider family and close, trusted friends. That love has been the revelation that has changed my life.

We finished Christmas Eve with a festive film – and it turned out to be a cracker called *Your Christmas or Mine?* I sometimes find Christmas movies rather overbearing or schmaltzy, but this gem hit the spot! It was funny, thoughtful and beautifully acted – but also very poignant given my situation. A father in the story is devastated after losing his wife several years earlier, and is all gruff and withdrawn. But another character brings him out of himself and helps him to realise that he has been neglecting his son, who is after all his biggest living connection with his wife. The obvious parallels with my story hit home. I could only wish that my father felt the same way about me... I let myself feel the pain of that, too. But then I reminded myself that sometimes there isn't redemption in life, as there is in a comforting film where you are pretty much assured of the happy ending. I couldn't force anyone else to choose a redemptive path in life, but I could choose it for myself. Which is what I have done, bit by bit, day by day.

The miracle was that, despite the tears and emotion, Christmas Eve ended well. I expressed what I needed to express, and then actually went to bed contented and slept well. And, looking back, Christmas Eve was by far my favourite day of the whole Christmas period.

Probably because of the emotions involved rather than despite them. I think there is something truly magical about Christmas Eve – the quiet expectancy, the building anticipation, the wonder of possibilities as Christmas Day approaches! I wish that I could hold onto it forever, that day that feels like a candle flickering in the darkness, gently lighting my way in a gloomy world, providing comfort and hope. But the truth is that its transience is part of its allure – there is no other day like it for me, and that is why I treasure it so.

And then suddenly we found ourselves in the bright dazzle of Christmas Day! A flurry of presents, fun, laughter, games, and far too much food. When else is it acceptable to have cake for breakfast?! Perhaps on one's birthday, but certainly the opportunities are few and far between!

We had decided to spend Christmas Day by ourselves this year, as I just wasn't sure how I would feel and I didn't want to impose any difficulties on other people at this time of year. We had a genuinely joyous time opening presents including one of those hilarious moments where you realise you have bought each other the same gift. We went for a long ramble during the traditional Christmas lunchtime, and on our return we made our feast – lots of our favourite foods, but planned to be easy to prepare. Aglow from our special meal, we sang carols and read Christmas Bible readings by firelight. We played card games with impractically large and unwieldy playing cards – because that is the kind of crazy thing you do on Christmas Day, right? The wonder of Christmas continued – I won my first game of clock solitaire, literally sitting cross-legged on the floor amongst the massive cards! Anyone who's played many rounds of that game knows that the odds of that happening are pretty slim...

But somehow Christmas Day wasn't quite as wonderful as Christmas Eve. There was nothing wrong with it and a lot that was great, but...if I'm honest, I've always found there to be something slightly anti-climactic about Christmas Day. The main events of the day happen so quickly, and then...well, you know you are on a downward slope and it is all coming to an end...which seems silly but it has always been the way it has felt to me. I used to cry bitter tears at the end of Christmas Day as a child, even when I knew that we would get up on Boxing Day and carry on having fun for several days, doing Christmassy things and eating Christmassy food. But somehow it just wasn't the same. Somehow it felt like the magical part was over, the candles were going out and the electric lights had been metaphorically turned back on in the world, and we were marching inexorably back to business as usual.

And yet here is the irony. The magic of Christmas Eve couldn't happen without the full glare and pinnacle that is Christmas Day. They are in a symbiotic relationship, and time marches on through Christmas Eve even though I would love nothing more than to grab hold of the moment and stay in it for far, far longer. But of course, it wouldn't feel the same if I could keep hold of it. There is something about the transient tenderness and expectancy of Christmas Eve that bestows upon it a peculiar and tantalising essence.

Chapter 14: What to do with the betwixt and between time?

What on earth happens between Christmas and New Year? It's a very odd time – one can lose track of days, see many different family members and friends, eat far more than is good for one. And of course, for many people work goes on. But somehow it doesn't feel like normal time.

We were meant to travel to see family for a couple of days after Christmas, but the weather defeated us. In the past, I would probably have found this highly dispiriting, but this time I was able to take it more in my stride. We found ourselves back at home with two more days by ourselves before my brother- and sister-in-law and their children arrived. We went for a long walk and, having travelled contentedly through a winter wonderland for at least an hour, we found ourselves in an open clearing in the forest – we looked at each other and both had the same idea. We knew that the snow that had fallen the previous week had been totally rubbish for snowman-building activities. More in hope than expectation, we both knelt down to ball up the snow and wait for it to fall apart...but it didn't! It was light, sticky and malleable. It turned out that the weather that had been treacherous for driving proved exceptional for snowman building – or, more precisely, snowlady building!

Thereby ensued one of the happiest Christmas times I can ever remember. We were able to build a snowlady who was the same height as me!! She had a proper head and a flowing body. We found perfect eye-shaped stones, a distinctive triangular stone for her nose, and a long piece of grass which gave her a perfectly endearing crooked smile. It was another piece of Christmas magic. I hugged her and felt truly joyful! It was hard to walk away from her and leave her there by herself, but somehow I knew she would be alright...just as I knew that I was going to be alright...

To be honest, we then had a more complicated period together. There was some misunderstanding, some unintended triggers, even a bit of marital squabbling. Isn't it odd how the most beautiful moments can be juxtaposed with more difficult periods sometimes? I have found that really hard in the past, as if the lovely moment has been polluted in my mind by the other stuff. This time we persevered through the challenges by talking together. It transpired that we both needed to be honest with ourselves that we were really, really tired. This healing process was working so well, but as well as being restorative it was also emotionally charged and quite physically sapping. We needed to be kinder to ourselves.

The next day, our visitors were due to arrive. A great thaw was taking place outside. I sometimes thought about our snowlady – isn't it odd how we think about snowmen as if they were real? Or is that just me...? I hadn't thought about returning to see her, but then Simon tentatively suggested it. We decided to go and pay her a visit, and see how she was doing in the higher temperatures. Impulsively, I picked up my cream scarf and flat cap as we walked out the door.

We weren't at all sure what to expect, a tad apprehensive as we climbed the hill towards where she had stood. As we rounded the corner, it was clear that she was still there – albeit considerably smaller. I had wondered if this might be the case, and had come prepared with a plan. With a few minutes' work, the snowlady became a snowchild, complete with hat and scarf. We hugged her, and felt profound. Again, it was hard to leave her, but I knew that she would be alright... just as I knew that little Alexandra was going to be alright...

This small act helped us to heal the events of the past twenty-four hours, and we went back home ready for the next few days of family madness and mayhem!

It was so important for us to have some family time and not just spend all of Christmas alone. Playing host and hostess was equal parts fun, rewarding and exhausting. All my careful meal planning paid off, ensuring that hungry nephews remained well fed. There were hilarious games, jokes, story-telling, and chases around the house. I wouldn't have changed it for the world, but there were barely any spare minutes in the day and, when those precious moments did come, all I could do was rest. I didn't say my Christmas affirmations or have any planned quiet time during that visit. But it was OK, because I was doing what I needed to do at that time, and I knew my affirmations so well that I could call upon one or more of them if I felt challenged by something. I was sustained and uplifted by all the work I had done up to that point. Situations which might have triggered a bad response from me in the past reoccurred but did not cause me the same angst. I felt far more in control of myself, and able to help myself when the inevitable challenges appeared. It was a lovely whirlwind of a time!

Chapter 15: New Year – the part I had forgotten about

I had been so focused on reclaiming Christmas that I had pretty much forgotten about New Year. In the past, I usually found this event tedious and underwhelming. Not being much of a late-night party type, normal New Year's Eve celebrations didn't really chime with me. But suddenly it was the day before New Year's Eve, and I felt a tug at my soul because of all the difficult things that had happened during the past year. I felt a bit blue, and I knew I needed to carve out some quality time for myself. I had to get up when no one else was awake in order to achieve this. It was hard to motivate myself to do this, but I knew deep down that it was necessary. I needed time to quieten myself, to process my thoughts, and to figure out how I was going to approach New Year's Eve.

The house was completely still and silent. I paused by our Christmas tree in the hallway and savoured the beauty of the pinpoint lights. I cleared the clutter from the living room and – guess what! – lit candles. I meditated and read daily Bible verses. I also felt drawn to poetry, which is not a medium I'm 100% comfortable with, so I have not generally sought it out. I have struggled to find the poetry that speaks to me amidst the reams of material that doesn't. But I figured that I had perhaps underestimated its power and so had recently bought a book offering a poem for each day of the year. This turned out to be an inspired idea, as it is helping to make poetry more accessible to me. It is opening my eyes to poets and genres of poetry that I would not easily have found by myself.

The night before New Year's Eve, several of the poems designated for the end of December and start of January spoke to me. Prospero from Shakespeare's *The Tempest*, musing on the profundity and shortness of life: "We are such stuff as dreams are made on, and our little life is rounded with a sleep." Lord Tennyson writing about New Year in *Ring Out, Wild Bells*, particularly these verses:

Ring out the old, ring in the new,
Ring, happy bells, across the snow;
The year is going, let him go;
Ring out the false, ring in the true.
Ring out the grief that saps the mind
For those that here we see no more;
Ring out the feud of rich and poor,
Ring in redress to all mankind.

And Charlotte Bronte's honest but upbeat poem, Life:

Life, believe, is not a dream
So dark as sages say;
Oft a little morning rain
Foretells a pleasant day.
Sometimes there are clouds of gloom,
But these are transient all;
If the shower will make the roses bloom,
O why lament its fall?
Rapidly, merrily,
Life's sunny hours flit by,

154

Gratefully, cheerily
Enjoy them as they fly!
What though Death at times steps in,
And calls our Best away?
What though sorrow seems to win,
O'er hope, a heavy sway?
Yet Hope again elastic springs,
Unconquered, though she fell;
Still buoyant are her golden wings,
Still strong to bear us well.
Manfully, fearlessly,
The day of trial bear,
For gloriously, victoriously,
Can courage quell despair!

I loved the notion of an elastic Hope rebounding after falling – so evocative of where I find myself at this point in my journey.

I also pondered the New Year tradition of making resolutions. There is a logic to this practice, but perhaps there is a prior step that we often choose to skip over, that of contemplating the year that has passed and picking out what we can celebrate from it, and what we can learn from it. This notion of New Year's Eve as a time to pause and contemplate really resonated with me. And yet it is incongruous with so many New Year traditions, which I generally find to be loud, gaudy and superstitious. In Spain, for example, people try to eat twelve green grapes during the time the clock strikes midnight to ward off bad luck. In Britain, we generally hold drunken parties and set off fireworks. I'm all for traditions and parties, but where is the real meaning in any of that?

I searched for any other rituals that I might find more in tune with how I felt. I was drawn to something that seems to be practised in different ways and places: along the lines of writing down things one wants to let go of from the year that is finishing, and things one hopes for in the New Year. Then burning that paper as a ceremonial way of letting go.

It was a seriously big moment for me, looking back on a year of tremendous upheaval and change, and looking forward to a year where our future is currently rather uncertain. I decided to ask Simon if he would be up for giving this ritual a go, and felt ready to go and grab some sleep before New Year's Eve officially began.

On New Year's Eve, we carved out ten minutes of quiet time together, and wrote our lists of what we wanted to let go of, and what we hoped for in the coming year. Then...the party started! All together, we played hilarious games that we had modified over the years to make them even more side-splitting – we no longer had any care who won, we just wanted to make each other cry with laughter! I think perhaps in the difficult months that had passed recently, I had temporarily forgotten just how healing and restorative genuine merriment can be. We lit a celebratory fire in the living room hearth, toasted marshmallows and drank mulled wine and warm juice. We took sparklers outside at about 10pm, and I used mine to spell the words Faith, Hope and Love. The sky was alight with its own sparklers – a breath-taking array of stars visible with the naked eye, and even more so through binoculars, and I particularly loved zoning in to see the individual stars in the cluster called the Pleiades.

We had no TV signal, so heralded in the New Year with the radio. As we tuned in about five minutes before midnight, they played a traditional Scottish song. The energy in the room quietened as we absorbed the gentle, reflective song which painted a picture of journeying together. I looked around the room and realised that this night was all about community. It was all about the family that I did have, not the family that I had lacked and lost. I heard the words "Choose life" going around and around in my head. As the chimes of Big Ben rang out over the airwaves, I lit a new candle and we all hugged. We said a simple prayer of dedication for the new year and then we danced the *Gay Gordons* around the living room floor. Then everyone reluctantly started heading for bed, having to admit that the sugar of the fire-toasted marshmallows would only keep us going for so long...

Simon and I came back to settle the last of the fire before bed. We found ourselves in a meditative state in front of the glowing fragments and logs, which looked as though they were alive. They were no longer aflame, but they were shimmering with latent heat and energy. As we broke up the logs, it was like watching a dancing, glowing community of molten nuggets. The pulsing light was mesmerising. I found myself thinking that the overarching summary of my recent Christmas journey was something like: "Focus on the light, and be together with those you truly love. Choose life."

Choose life indeed. It is something we have to keep doing consciously every day. Don't let the darkness win. Be the light. Spread the light. Tend your flame so that it burns ever brighter and stronger.

Despite going to bed after midnight on New Year's Eve, I was determined to get up early to walk up the hill behind our house for sunrise on New Year's Day. My awesome hubby agreed to curtail his well-earned rest to join me! We crept out of the house while the others slept, and walked by the light of my phone along paths and through fields. The land sparkled with a hard frost – everything glimmered. As light slowly grew in the sky, I saw that it was more overcast than I had hoped for – no glorious sunrise likely today – but I find there is something truly special about being up and about when the vast majority of humanity is in bed. I can usher in the first dawn of the New Year in my own quiet, reflective way.

As we walked up the hill, I recalled one of the things my husband had written down the previous day which he wanted us to let go. He wanted us to stop talking about my father on our walks. I had asked him more about that before we tossed our papers onto the fire. He had said that it was natural that I had often reflected on the situation with my father while walking during the past year, but he had several memories of walks in beautiful places where we had needed to stop to compose ourselves after a traumatic conversation. All of that had been necessary, but he hoped that it would not be necessary forever.

I found his observation so insightful. I have a habit of ruminating on things while I walk. This can often be incredibly cathartic, but sometimes one can just keep ruminating out of habit. Keep returning to the old wounds. I had kept asking myself why my father acted the way he did, why things had turned out the way they had. While some contemplation of these questions had proved illuminating on my healing journey, continually returning to something that has no concrete, knowable answer is not ultimately helpful.

As I walked up the hill and enjoyed the still view from the top, I vowed not to talk about my father so much, on walks or otherwise. I also vowed to halt my internal monologue on the subject as well. This was not about suppressing emotions or thoughts, but rather about breaking a ruminating habit. I felt I was ready to move on now. Ready to focus on the future rather than constantly rehashing and questioning the past. Ready to make a New Year's resolution to myself. We only have a certain amount of energy and time on this earth, and I'm ready to devote mine to building my dreams.

This was honestly the best New Year I have ever experienced. It was meaningful, it was spent with family whom I love, and it was joyous. It was not pre-planned and it somewhat took me by surprise, but it built on everything else I had focused on up to that point.

"Focus on the light and be together with those you love. Stop ruminating on the past. Choose life. Choose your dreams." What better advice could I give myself going into a new year?

Chapter 16: The end of the season

I have always found the process of taking down Christmas decorations to be distinctly depressing. All the lovely, shiny stuff is packed away, leaving behind the dreary, dark coldness of early January. Why can't we just keep on celebrating and let the decorations stay up?

Interestingly, that is exactly what my husband and I did in early 2021. During those lonely days of lockdown, we decided that it would be uplifting to keep the decorations up. I don't think we were alone in that idea. And it worked, up to a point. I loved continuing to enjoy the sparkling lights and brightly coloured decorations. However, after a while I got used to them and they had hardly any effect on me. It just felt like they had been up too long, and a sense of staleness took over. And we had no obvious timetable to help us decide when to take the decorations down anymore, so they stayed up for quite a while.

I believe that the transience of the Christmas season lends it much of its magic. If we try to hold onto it for too long, it loses its freshness. But I'm determined not to end the season on a low note this year. There has to be a better way.

We had decided to take our decorations down after work on January 5th. The day did not start auspiciously. A couple of stressful situations that we had managed to box away over Christmas were rearing their ugly heads again, and my husband and I both felt upset at the same time. Always a recipe for things to get complicated. I may even have smashed a mug full of mint tea... Quite satisfying to be honest, but not a sign of being in a mentally great place. We both improved during the morning as we got on with work. But I worried that we wouldn't feel positive enough to make a good fist of putting the decorations away in the evening. Maybe we would have to postpone to the next day, but I really didn't want to. I wanted to bite the bullet.

As it turned out, in another sign that my ability to handle my moods is improving with all this intentional practice, things were in a much better place by the afternoon and evening. We went ahead and took down the decorations. We considered this as a meaningful ritual rather than a depressing task, which meant approaching it with attention and intention. Attention so that we weren't simply getting it over with as quickly as possible. And intention so that we would think carefully about how we were doing the task.

Perspective was vital. I could remember that there is still beauty to be found in the world after the Christmas decorations have gone away, and in fact it is up to me to find and generate that beauty.

I needed to be able to accept things as they were and live in the moment – not trying to grasp onto and artificially prolong what was. Whereas animals naturally live in the moment, for humans the by-product of a more advanced brain is the tendency to dwell on past events and endlessly worry about different permutations of what might happen in the future. Coming back to the moment and fully experiencing its richness is a core tenet of wellbeing.

And most fundamentally in this case, the key was gratitude. Instead of mourning that Christmas was passed, we turned the putting away of the decorations into a ritual of thanksgiving. We said a short prayer at the start, expressing our thankfulness that Christmas had indeed been a miraculous time of reclaiming, redemption and healing. We then took our time putting away the decorations, chatting to each other along the way about fun things we remembered about our Christmas. We laughed and reminisced, and it elevated a mundane – and potentially sad – task into a joyful experience. We chortled at how the artificial Christmas tree and the strings of fairy lights stood absolutely no chance of properly fitting back into their original boxes. This was a million miles away from the stressed and depressed Alexandra who used to rush the job and get annoyed and upset in the process.

I also wanted to end the ritual on a positive note. Happy music and dancing had been hugely beneficial for me during this Christmas period, and there was no reason why we couldn't carry that forward into the new year, just with non-Christmassy music.

Now, this is the moment where you may suspect that I'm making this up to give the book a memorable ending!! I can totally understand why you would think that, but I can assure you this next bit is 100% true. As my husband wrestled with the storage cupboard to put away the final boxes of decorations, I was looking through my music collection. I had a couple of ideas of upbeat songs we could dance to, but neither of them felt quite right. I remembered that we had particularly enjoyed Meghan Trainor's Christmas album, and that there were a couple of her non-Christmas songs that we also found fun, so I navigated to that part of my music library. What I discovered were two songs I had purchased in the past but long forgotten – songs Meghan had recorded for The Peanuts Movie.

Good to be alive and *Better when I'm dancin'*.

They were utterly perfect, in the way they got us dancing around but also for the messages they contained. Messages of dancing freely to express ourselves, and of living in the moment to savour life. Although I can't explain it, I truly believe there are moments when God/the Universe gives you a perfect gift of exactly what you need at that time. This was one of those moments. Simon and I boogied away like no one was watching, and thankfully, no one was!

Closing thoughts

I can honestly say that I have reclaimed and redeemed Christmas through this experiment. At times I was scared that it would all fall down around my ears, but it didn't. And magic happened.

I have a few final reflections on this time which may help you if you have a similar journey ahead of you.

Take the time that you need. I found that I needed to honour this particular part of my healing journey with a lot of time. I was away from work for three weeks over the Christmas period and had plenty of time to myself. I recognise that is a luxury one is not often afforded in life – but I think it is necessary to give yourself the requisite time and space you need at these pivotal moments. If you try to multitask too much, you will almost certainly come a-cropper. The heart and the mind need to be able to breathe and process at a gentle pace.

Be kind to yourself. This sort of journey will take lots of energy. You will need to rest. You will need to prioritise yourself more than usual. You will need to give yourself good things to nourish and replenish your soul. Give yourself what you would freely give to a close friend in a similar situation. Allow yourself to put yourself first.

Find creative material to support you and ignite your spark. I've explored music, dance, short stories and poetry during this period, and have found extraordinary comfort and inspiration that I wasn't expecting. There is power in creative expression of all kinds. There is power in knowing that others have trodden a similar path to you. And there is power in hearing and feeling someone else's perspective on that path, which allows new understanding to blossom.

Learn to listen to and follow your intuition. I'm convinced that our true inner voices can be incredible guides for us, helping us to know what to do and when, in order to heal. We just need to learn to listen to that voice carefully, to give it space so that we can hear its quiet wisdom. It takes practice, but it is so worth it.

And so I leave you with my hopes for you – at Christmas and in your wider life:

May you be richly blessed on your personal journey.

May you hear that wonderful, quiet voice of wisdom that will guide you on your way.

May you be creative and bold to try new practices, to unearth what works best for you.

May you liberate your thinking mind, your emotional mind, your body, and your spirit.

May you be wise to know when to let go of things, and when to reclaim them.

May you find overflowing healing, peace, joy and love.

May you reach the destination that has seemed unattainable for so long.

May you rest and sing and dance and love.

May you grow to be fully you.

Epilogue

I wrote this book at Christmas 2022. Now, as I review it a short half-year later, a great deal has happened.

In March, I took the plunge and handed in my notice on my well-paying day job. I still had three months of notice to serve, but I had taken the big decision to focus on my dream. My dream to set up my own business to support other people's mental health and wellbeing: Damsel Not In Distress Ltd!

I have been taking steps to launch my business for about a year now. My mission is to guide people on their path to liberation and peace, so they can discover and achieve their higher purpose in life. Alongside this, I am passionate about raising awareness of emotional abuse – what it is, how it affects people, and how they can set themselves free and find peace.

Then, in June, my world turned upside down. My father was found dead inside his home. As well as being estranged from me, his only living relative, he had cut off ties with pretty much everyone. He had seemingly achieved what he had declared to me many times in recent years was his intention: to drink himself to death.

I'm still processing what has happened.

To say that this has been a complicated journey is an understatement. My story of hurt stretches for more than forty years, and my story of healing has spanned twenty years, and is now finally reaching its conclusion. I will tell more of this story in due course, but for now suffice it to say that I am firmly directing my gaze to the future, to helping others, and to continuing to journey towards the light.

Come and find me online – I so look forward to meeting you!
My website: https://www.damselnotindistress.co.uk
Facebook: https://www.facebook.com/damselnotindistressltd
Instagram: https://www.instagram.com/damsel_notin_distress/

I've also put together *Your Ideal Christmas Present*, a five-day video course designed to help you reconnect with what you really love about Christmas. It's free! Please do visit my website at https://www.damselnotindistress.co.uk/xmasfreebie to get hold of it.

References

Cohen G.L., and Sherman D.K. (2014). The psychology of change: self-affirmation and social psychological intervention. Annu Rev Psychol. 65:333-71. doi: 10.1146/annurev-psych-010213-115137. PMID: 24405362.

Elkjaer, E., Mikkelsen, M. B., Michalak, J., Mennin, D. S., and O'Toole, M. S. (2022). Expansive and Contractive Postures and Movement: A Systematic Review and Meta-Analysis of the Effect of Motor Displays on Affective and Behavioral Responses. Perspectives on Psychological Science, 17(1), 276-304. https://doi.org/10.1177/1745691620919358

Wood, J. V., Perunovic, W. Q. E., and Lee, J. W. (2009). Positive Self Statements: Power for some, peril for others. Association for Psychological Science, 20(7), 860-866.

About the Author

Alexandra Walker is a life coach, author and musician.

She ostensibly had the dream life. Graduating top of her class at university in 2002, getting a doctorate in applied mathematics in 2006, and showing her musical talent by performing Grieg's piano concerto and writing and producing a musical. Then rising to leadership positions in the civil service and charitable sector in the heart of London for 15 years.

But she was profoundly unhappy and unwell. It would be a long journey until her eyes were opened to the emotional abuse that had dogged her entire life.

An accredited member of ACCPH, Alexandra has set up her business, Damsel Not In Distress Ltd, to guide others on their path to liberation, peace and their higher purpose in life.

She now lives in the North West Highlands of Scotland with her husband Simon. They love exploring the hills, and finished climbing the 282 Scottish Munros in 2021.

Printed in Great Britain
by Amazon

30635757R00099